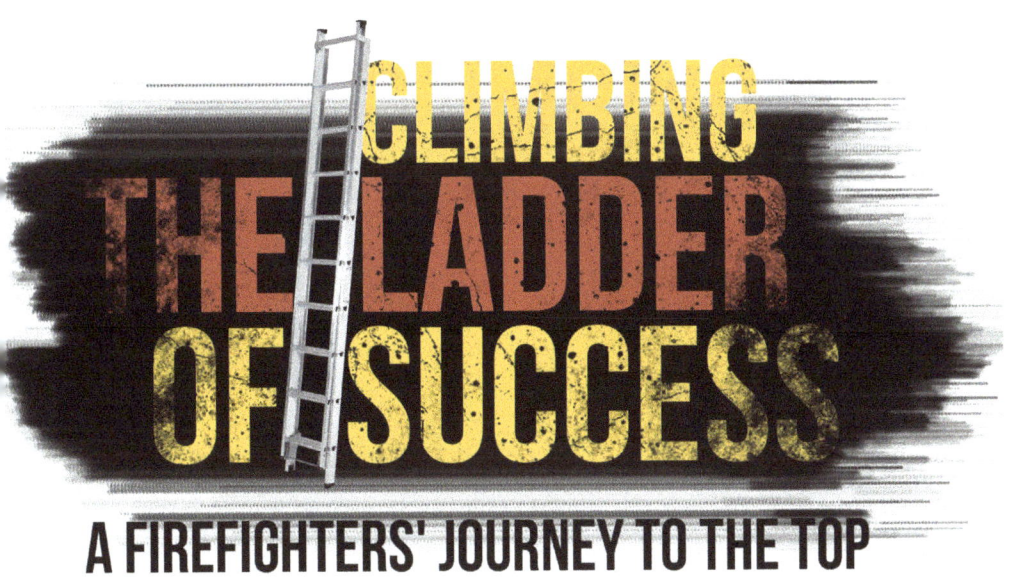

A FIREFIGHTERS' JOURNEY TO THE TOP

RAWLEIGH QUARLES, SR.

outskirts
press

Climbing the Ladder of Success: A Firefighters' Journey to the Top
All Rights Reserved.
Copyright © 2022 Rawleigh Quarles, Sr.
v4.0

The opinions expressed in this manuscript are solely the opinions of the author and do not represent the opinions or thoughts of the publisher. The author has represented and warranted full ownership and/or legal right to publish all the materials in this book.

This book may not be reproduced, transmitted, or stored in whole or in part by any means, including graphic, electronic, or mechanical without the express written consent of the publisher except in the case of brief quotations embodied in critical articles and reviews.

Outskirts Press, Inc.
http://www.outskirtspress.com

ISBN: 978-1-9772-5024-7

Cover & interior images © 2022 Rawleigh Quarles, Sr. All rights reserved - used with permission.

Outskirts Press and the "OP" logo are trademarks belonging to Outskirts Press, Inc.

PRINTED IN THE UNITED STATES OF AMERICA

Dedication

To my adorable wife Barbara and our three wonderful children Rawleigh Jr, Derrick, and Nicole who each were supportive, encouraging, and understanding during my experience as well as in the writing of this book, not to mention their sacrifices and their dedication, without which, none of this would have been possible. May this book help to keep alive an awareness of the great sacrifices required to achieve racial equality and the elimination of racial bias, racial discrimination, and racial injustice everywhere.

Thanks for taking this incredible journey with me. Your love, support and encouragement made all the difference during my more than 31+ years of service to the citizens of the City of Roanoke. It was an honor to have served in this area of dedicated and humble service in my quest for justice and equality for all mankind. Your faith in God and me and my faith in God and you, served as my source of strength and determination.

Table of Contents

Preface i
A Special Thanks To v
Acknowledgements vii
Introduction.. ix
About the Author xi
1. Early Childhood Desire and Wonderment............................ 1
2. Hopes, Dreams, and Aspirations Becomes a Reality 5
3. Life in the Fire Station 15
4. Life in the Community as a Firefighter............................ 20
5. Rookie Mistakes or Just Setup? 25
6. A Candlemakers' Nightmare 27
7. The Lull Before the Storm 31
8. The Equal Employment Opportunity Commission (EEOC) Determines Roanoke City Fire Department Biased: Quarles Wins Job Discrimination Suit...................................... 38
9. Fire Code Enforcement and Politics............................... 47
10. Arbitrarily Transferred from the Fire Marshal's Office............... 56
11. All Glory, Honor, Thanks, and Praise Belongs to God for Allowing Me to Climb the Ladder of Success and Reach My Journey to the Top.. 69

12. Confirmation or Validation of God's Divine Call to
    Proclaim the Word of God or to the Preaching Ministry.......... 86
13. Fire Chief Announces Retirement... 91
14. After Reaching the Top, What Now?! The Best
    Was Yet to Come! 147

Preface

This book was written following my 31+ years employment with the City of Roanoke (Virginia) Fire Department, now the Roanoke Fire-EMS Department. After more than twenty-six years into retirement, I was motivated to share my story in a written autobiography of the biases, discrimination, prejudices, and racial injustices I encountered while climbing the ladder of success. This book is an attempt to inform the readers of the encumbrances, difficulties, stumbling blocks, and outright injustices that I and other minorities encountered and still encounter in our quest to succeed.

Writing this book has been one of the most exciting challenges of my life. I am thankful for the privilege to have been chosen to be a drum major for justice, and to have endured the struggle to achieve justice and equality for others coming after me.

It was written for the purpose of shining light on and exposing the cultural and racial bias that has always existed, and still does today in our society, regarding the discriminatory practices, methods, tactics, and illegalities against people of color regarding hiring and promotions in all workforce categories. This has been, and still is an ongoing and deliberate attempt to promote the advancement of whites over people of color and to prevent the advancement of people of color. This racial injustice is still "alive and well" on the local, state, and national level today, and in particularly in our fire and police departments.

I experienced life changing events during my 31+ years experience as I struggled to climb the ladder of success in an effort to reach the top. As a result of my fight for justice and racial equality, I became a drum major for justice.

This book conveys real life experiences in the life of a firefighter, beginning with my childhood desire to become a firefighter, my hopes, my dreams, my desires, and my aspirations as a firefighter. The chapters in this book convey the following: Early Childhood Desire and Wonderment, Hopes, Dreams, and Aspirations Becomes a Reality, Life in the Fire Station, Life in the Community as a Firefighter, Rookies Mistakes or Just Set Up, A Candlemakers' Nightmare, The Lull Before the Storm, The Equal Employment Opportunity Commission (EEOC) Determines Roanoke City Fire Department Biased: Quarles Wins Job Discrimination Suit, Fire Code Enforcement and Politics, Arbitrarily Transferred from the Fire Marshal's Office, All Glory, Honor, Thanks, and Praise Belongs to God for Allowing Me to Climb the Ladder of Success and Reach My Journey to the Top, Confirmation or Validation of God's Divine Call to Proclaim the Word of God or to the Preaching Ministry, Fire Chief Announces Retirement, and After Reaching the Top, What Now?! The Best Was Yet to Come.

The main character in this book is the author (which is me), but there are other unidentified and unnamed individuals without which, the writing of this book would not have been possible.

It is my intent and sole purpose to convey to the readers, the devastating effect and impact this injustice and discrimination has on our society and the entire nation. Injustice and discrimination anywhere, is injustice and discrimination everywhere. It is also my sincere hope and prayer that in your quest for success and achievement, that you recognize and confront any and all tactics, schemes, stratagems, and outright blatant acts of discrimination that you may encounter, and that without fear of reprisal, harassment, threats, intimidation, politics, and politicians, that you pursue your constitutional rights, liberties, and justice that everyone is constitutionally promised and entitled to. All glory, honor, and praise belong to God, for His grace and mercy through it all.

A Special Thanks To

My most adorable and loving wife Barbara, who truly is a blessing from the Lord. Thank you for your loyal and faithful support, as the wife of a fire department employee, while I endured my struggles of racial injustice and politics of the profession. All of your trials and stressors of the profession that you endured, just prepared you for your greatest challenges yet to come in your life. Those challenges were, serving as the First Lady of the church that elected me to serve as pastor. You rose to the occasion in both the challenges that you faced, and you excelled in them, by going above and beyond the call of duty. No one, and I mean no one, could have equaled or surpassed you. I am very proud of you for your support, your love, and for always being by my side. You are to be praised for your accomplishments.

Acknowledgements

Special thanks to my most wonderful, adoring, and loving wife Barbara and my daughter Nicole Martinez, who were instrumental and encouraging to me to write this book over the many years since my retirement. Without their support and encouragement, I would have never undertaken such a task as this. Words are inadequate to express my sincere appreciation and for their undying devotion regarding the writing of this autobiography. To my grandson Alejandro Martinez, a special thanks, who was also instrumental in assisting me with photography, scanning, formatting, editing, cropping, cutting, designing advertising flyers and posters, setting up news conferences for television, newspaper, and radio, the scheduling of several book signings, and the compilation of information that had been stored and arranged in large document albums, covering the span of my 31+ year career.

Introduction

The purpose of this book is to provide the reader with information that addresses and exposes racial barriers, as well as other aspects of discrimination and bias that exist even today in our society as a whole, and particularly, those encountered or experienced in fire and police departments across the nation. It is also the authors' intent to reveal his personal experience of such racial bias and discrimination during his 31+ year career with the City of Roanoke Fire Department. "Climbing the Ladder of Success: A Firefighters' Journey to the Top" identifies personal, as well as corporate bias in all levels of employment (government as well as private) and should also hopefully challenge each of us to take a firm position that racial injustice anywhere will result in racial injustice everywhere.

We are living in the 21st century and laws have been passed, prohibiting all seven types of employment discrimination which are: Race Discrimination, Color Discrimination, National Origin Discrimination, Sex Discrimination, Military Discrimination, Military Status, and Retaliation.

Specifically, the acts of discrimination in the workplace are identified as employment discrimination. Employment discrimination generally exist where an employer treats an applicant or employee less favorably merely, because of a person's race, color, religion, sex, sexual orientation, gender identity, national origin, disability, or status as a protected veteran.

It is hoped that justice and equality prevail whenever these laws have been violated which deprives an individual of his or her rights and entitlement to life, liberty, and the pursuit of happiness.

About the Author

Dr. Rawleigh W. Quarles, Sr. is senior pastor of the Staunton Avenue Church of God in Roanoke, Virginia. He has served in this capacity since 1994 for a period of twenty-nine years. Prior to his divine call to proclaim/preach the Word of God, he was employed by the City of Roanoke Fire Department for more than 31+ years. He elected to take early retirement in 1995 for full time ministry and proclamation of the gospel of Jesus Christ. He is a graduate of the National Fire Academy in Emmitsburg, Maryland as an Executive Fire Officer. Dr. Quarles has numerous college courses related to fire science from the college of William and Mary in Williamsburg, Virginia, Virginia Polytechnic Institute (VPI) in Blacksburg, Virginia, and Virginia Western Community College (VWCC) in Roanoke, Virginia. He was appointed to serve a two-year term on the Virginia Fire Services Board (now Virginia Fire Commission) in 1982-1984, by Governor Charles A. Robb. He was also appointed to serve a second term of four years, on the Virginia Fire Services Board (Virginia Fire Commission) in 1992-1995, by Governor Lawrence Douglas Wilder. Dr. Quarles received the Key to the City of Roanoke, Virginia in 1995 from the office of the mayor, a Mayoral Proclamation in 1962 from the City of Roanoke, Virginia, office of the mayor, proclaiming Saturday, May 4, 2012 throughout this great all-American city, as "Rawleigh and Barbara Quarles Day," and a second Mayoral Proclamation in 1995, from the City of Roanoke, Virginia, office of the mayor, proclaiming Saturday, April 8, 1995 throughout this great all-American City as "Rawleigh W. Quarles, Sr. Day." He is also the recipient of many other awards, certificates of recognition, and plaques for outstanding service and contributions on the local and state level. He also received two honorary doctorate degrees from the Bethlehem Bible College of Roanoke, Virginia. The Honorary Doctorate Degree in Theology and the Honorary Doctorate Degree in Humane Letters.

CHAPTER 1

Early Childhood Desire and Wonderment

It was in the year of 1954 at the age of twelve while growing up in the northeast section of Roanoke City that I had a desire to be a firefighter in the Roanoke City Fire Department. Although I was not old enough to be employed by the city much less be a firefighter, I often wondered why I never saw minorities, blacks, or people of color working as firefighters when they were in my neighborhood or any neighborhood extinguishing fires, filling on-board water tanks, and servicing fire hydrants.

Even at the young age of twelve, I could not comprehend why all the faces of the firefighters were white. I realize now, looking back, that I was too young and naïve to be aware of the cultural shock that I was later awakened to of the existing bias, racial discrimination, and racial injustice that was alive and well in the Roanoke City Government as well as city, county, state, and federal governments everywhere.

I remember watching with childhood fascination whenever fires were extinguished in my neighborhood. In particular, I would observe from my front yard, firefighters filling their water tanks from the fire hydrant located on the corner in front of my house. Over and over again, each time this would occur, I was always left with the same question, "why no blacks?" This longing desire continued for the next nine years before my hopes, dreams, and aspirations became a reality.

Before graduation from high school in 1960, while I was in my early teens, I worked after school, on Saturdays and during the summer for several years in a neighborhood grocery store as a clerk and grocery delivery boy. My second job just before graduation was also in a neighborhood grocery store as a clerk and grocery delivery boy.

My third job was with a building construction crew supervised by my brother John from the age of twelve until the age of eighteen during the summer months and on Saturdays. My job entailed finishing the interior of dwellings under construction with sheet rock, lathe, rock wool insulation, and metal corner angles and edges before the plasterers would plaster the building.

After graduation, I was employed at a laundry and dry cleaners as a part time laundry worker and part time chauffer for the owner of the business. I remained at the laundry and dry cleaners for approximately three years before I was hired by the City of Roanoke Fire Department as a firefighter in 1963.

Getting started

Nobody forgets the lessons they learned on the very first job

By JOE KENNEDY
STAFF WRITER

We all had to start someplace.

Whether it was scooping cones in an ice cream store, handling rods for a surveying crew or driving a truck for a dry cleaner, we began our working lives as eager young people with a lot to learn.

Some of us stayed in the fields we first chose. Others went on to much different things. But the lessons stayed with us and, no doubt, helped steer us toward the jobs we have now.

For Labor Day, several Roanoke Valley residents recall their first jobs.

□ □

Name: Rawleigh Quarles.
Position: Roanoke Fire Chief.
First job: Full-time summer helper at Northside Grocery at 12th Street and Loudon Avenue in Roanoke at age 16.
Pay: $40 to $50 per week.

In the grocery business, young Rawleigh Quarles did it all. "I drove a pickup truck to Associated Grocers in Salem," he says. "I cut meat, worked the cash register, waited on customers and even carried groceries to people's houses. I'd go out on Saturdays with three or four different truckloads."

The experience taught him how to develop a rapport with customers and how to handle money, stock shelves, conduct an inventory and order supplies.

Quarles, 49, stayed on at the store after graduating from Lucy Addison High School. That same year, he took a job at the Ideal Laundry and then was hired as a city firefighter.

He became chief in 1989.

Quarles' rise to the top wasn't always smooth. He filed a racial discrimination complaint against the city in the 1970s and won a promotion to fire marshal and

FROM PAGE 1
$14,000 in back pay.

The keys to his struggle have been "hard work, determination, perseverance, preparation, stick-to-itiveness and the ability and desire to do well and advance."

□ □

2 Negroes Among 6 Firemen To Begin Training In City

Six new firemen—including the first Negroes ever hired by the department—are undergoing basic training in fighting fires.

The men, who go on duty Jan. 1, will be on probation for a year of intensive training after that.

Right now they are learning such basic skills as hooking hoses to hydrants, using the proper nozzles and finding and using equipment on trucks.

Fire Chief Sidney W. Vaughan said the men will train this month at various stations throughout the city. Today and tomorrow they are assigned to No. 10 station.

Two more men have been hired, but are having trouble with paper work. They are expected to be on training duty by Monday.

Vaughan said eight other men should also go on duty soon, perhaps Monday. They have passed written tests and are undergoing physical examinations.

Vaughan said the second group does not include any Negroes. He said he sent letters to five Negroes, but the two on duty were the only ones to pass the written tests administered by the Virginia Employment Commission.

Two of the men are normal replacements for the department. The other 14 are to compensate for the man hours which will be lost when the department goes on a shorter duty week Jan. 1.

Eight others will be hired in the spring when the Garden City station opens.

The Negro members of the training group are Joseph Calvin Crutchfield of 820 Fairfax Ave., NW, and Raleigh Wendell Quarles of 2011 Gandy Drive, NW.

Crutchfield is a former insurance salesman and Quarles worked for a local laundry.

The other new men are David Rich of 115 Ninth St., SE, who transferred to the fire department from the city sewage treatment plant; Donald E. Tinsley of Rt. 10, Roanoke, a former Salem fireman who plans to move to city soon; Donald R. Haw of 2630 Vancouver Drive, N a former employe of D mond Plastics; and Freder G. Jackson of 1462 Gre brier Ave., SE, a former e ploye of Swift Packing Co.

Capt. D. R. Sink is charge of their training.

Capt. D. R. Sink watches Quarles (center and Rich operate nozzle

CHAPTER 2

Hopes, Dreams, and Aspirations Becomes a Reality

On December 1, 1963, the City of Roanoke's bastion or the "last private white man's club" was integrated or de-segregated. This "club" was known as the City of Roanoke Fire Department. The city was compelled to hire minority firefighters within its ranks, and as a result of this decision, two minorities were hired and sworn in as firefighters for the City of Roanoke Fire Department, thus ending racial discrimination, racial bias, and racial injustice regarding fire department employment.

There was an article printed in the Roanoke Times and World News quoting a firefighter as saying (regarding the hiring of minorities), "I will work with them, but I will not eat and sleep with them." There were no sudden and unexpected resignations following the departments integration. I was one of the two minorities hired as a firefighter.

Remember, I said (regarding the department's integration or hiring), this ended the departments discrimination in hiring, but discrimination in promotional opportunities still existed and surfaced later. I will always remember so vividly the racially biased obstacles I encountered and had to overcome to even be selected by the chief as a firefighter. Little did anyone suspect that this was the initial exposure and dismantling of racial bias and discrimination that existed in the fire department and the City of Roanoke as a whole. This racially biased, discriminatory, and racial injustice that existed in this "last private white man's club" had never before been challenged.

Of course, I was assigned to Fire Station No. 1, Fire Department Headquarters in the downtown district, where else? I'm sure this decision was made to minimize trouble that may occur if I had been assigned to an outlying station, and of course, to keep an eye on me.

The new applicants (which included me) were all required to take an Aptitude Test and only those successfully passing would be eligible for selection by the Fire Chief. How convenient was that for systematic discrimination?! I was only one of two minorities to be selected for induction into the "last white man's private club" as a member.

Within days after my employment, firefighters began asking me what type of test I had to take. I related to them that it was an Aptitude Test and they each stated that they had not been required to take any test. In fact, they did not even know what an Aptitude Test was. What does that tell you? Some of the firefighters were recently hired just before me but were never required to take a test to be employed. This test was used initially for the first time as a qualifier or disqualifier for minority applicants. Prior to this test, applicants were chosen solely at the discretion of the Fire Chief. Needless to say, there were instances where nepotism had occurred.

2 Negroes To Become City Firemen

Pending final health reports due later today, eight new firemen will go on duty Monday with the Roanoke Fire Department.

Two of them are Negroes, the first in the department.

Fire Chief Sidney W. Vaughan said the eight were chosen on the basis of tests and interviews. The city health department is expected to give its final report on the eight men later today.

Another group of eight new men will probably report for duty Dec. 9, Vaughan said, after undergoing a battery of tests.

Fourteen of the men are being hired to reduce the department's duty week from 73 to 68 hours beginning Jan. 1. The other two are to fill vacancies, Vaughan said.

The 16 new men will receive a month's training at stations throughout the city in operation of ladders, hoses, pumps and other techniques.

They will go on actual duty as firemen Jan. 1.

Still another group of eight men will be hired early next year to man the new station in Garden City now under construction.

9 More Firemen Begin Training

Nine more rookies reported to the Roanoke Fire Department today to begin their training.

Fire Chief Sidney W. Vaughan said another man has been notified to report for duty Dec. 16.

They will join six other men who began training last week and all will go on regular duty Jan. 1.

Fourteen of the men will make up the duty hours needed to permit firemen to go on a 68-hour week beginning next month. They now are on duty roughly 73 hours. The other two men filled vacancies in the department.

The trainees include the first two Negroes ever hired by the department.

—World-News Photos by Oakie Asbu
Hose forms pattern in front of dwelling

Home's Slow Burn Teaching Recruits Fireman's Trade

Roanoke firemen are battling flames at a frame house, but they don't expect to save it.

In fact, they expect to have it burned to the ground by Friday.

The two-story residence is the property of the Virginia Highway Department, and the firemen are setting it on fire to train the new men added to the department this month.

The house on Hart Avenue, just east of Booker T. Washington Junior High School, must make way for construction of Interstate Spur 581. So the firemen were given permission to use it for practice.

The eight rookies on duty today repeatedly rushed into the house to find the fires set by Fire Chief Sidney W. Vaughan and Capt. D. R. Sink, department drillmaster.

Outside they worked under the direction of Capt. S. L. Lovelace. A department veteran, D. A. Yopp, operated the water pumper for the hoses.

The department had an opportunity to burn quite a few houses several years ago during the clearance of the Commonwealth Redevelopment Project, Lovelace said. But this is the first house available in some time.

He said practice in a house under real fire conditions is one of the best possible experiences for new men. The rookies have to trace the smoke to its source, then extinguish the flames as rapidly as possible.

But some of the fires today were so extensive, they could be readily seen from outside.

Eight other rookies on tomorrow's shift will practice on the house then. The house, which is already patched with scorch marks, will be used as long

Flames leap into wall as it holds out during the week.

The men fighting the fires today were David Rich, Rawleigh Quarles, Ronald Ragland, Douglas Dixon, Gerald Wells, Maurice Holt, Richard Sarver and Charles Snyder.

Quarles and Rich head for the house on the run

The Roanoke World-News

Monday, January 27, 1964

CHAPTER 3

Life in the Fire Station

Work hours for fire suppression personnel (firefighters) were three twenty-four-hour shifts, every other day (twenty-four hours on duty and twenty-four hours off duty) and then seventy-two hours off after the third day of work. That was quite an adjustment from the normal forty-hour work week. For the most part firefighters were on their best behavior. The day before I reported for duty, the fire chief called me and the only other black firefighter hired along with me into his office for a meeting. He said to us, "there may be times that you might hear racial terms from your brother firefighters." I should have responded with, "are you kidding?"

Realizing that my presence in the department would have an impact regarding the acceptance of other minority firefighters coming after me, I decided early on to set the highest standard of conduct to assure their smooth induction and acceptance into the department, not to mention their future achievement, promotions, and advancement. Recognizing this, suddenly brought to bear on me the weight on my shoulders of being a role model for others in their quest for racial equality and racial justice. It seemed to me like the world was watching me under a microscope.

Again, let me reiterate for the record, that for the most part, the firefighters were on their "best behavior" and tried not to use derogatory and racially and ethnically charged terms in my presence. But its hard to suppress deliberate racial bigotry after many years of what is considered and accepted as the norm in our culture and society.

When it was time to kick back, relax, chill, unwind, recline, and watch tv, I just have to relate to you of the sometimes and often frequent use of the racist remarks, and the racially charged atmosphere that existed. At both stations where I had worked, I was the only African American among sixteen or seventeen white firefighters. Needless to say, democracy was never on my side nor in my favor. The television program selections were usually three, country music, country music, or more country music. Take your choice. I was never down for any of the three choices. I remember one Saturday morning in particular, I was the first and only person viewing the television, and a black musical show was airing when suddenly, all the other firefighters entered the room and after a few minutes, without warning, and in total disregard and disrespect for me, a firefighter walked up to the television, turned the station, and said, "that's enough of that nigger shit."

While participating in an in-station drill regarding the location of fire alarm boxes throughout the city, and the testing and maintenance of these boxes, someone asked the Drill Instructor about the frequency of testing these boxes, and the Drill Instructors' response was "that's ok, them niggers will test them for you," (he was referring to black people). Thus, indicating that only black people pulled false fire alarms.

If you have never hung out or spent a considerable amount of time at a fire station as a civilian, you can't begin to appreciate the camaraderie and mischievousness that takes place between fellow firefighters. There are times when pranks, jokes, and horseplay even involve civilians. Let me share with you two different incidents that involved a young boy around eleven years of age at one of the stations where I was assigned.

On one occasion, he came to the station to buy a loaf of bread and other items from the station store. While he was shopping, one of the firefighters (the station clown and prankster), decided to have some fun with him. The plan was put into action to distract him and ask him to place his loaf of bread on the apparatus floor just under the opening in the ceiling of the second floor where the sliding pole extended from the first floor up through the ceiling and anchored to the ceiling of the second floor. The shopper would then be distracted, while leaving his loaf of bread unattended on the floor at the bottom of the sliding pole, while a firefighter would slide the pole thus landing on the loaf of bread crushing it. You may have guessed what happened after that. When the firefighter landed, the loaf of bread was completely flattened and to add insult to injury, another firefighter began kicking what was left of the flattened loaf of bread until it was completely crushed. Slices of bread were strewn all over the station floor. The young boy began to cry and ran from the station with the remaining slices of bread and along the way, his remaining slices of bread were strewn through the station behind him. What a blast! Just before he completely exited the station, his loaf of bread was replaced.

On another occasion, guess who? Same station, same players, same prankster, and the same victim. The young boy was asked to stand on the apparatus floor, just under the same hole as before. While he was being distracted by a firefighter talking to him, another firefighter would be standing on the second floor with a bucket of water and at just the right moment, the firefighter would move away from the victim leaving him all alone under the pole opening, when suddenly, a bucket of water was poured from the second floor drenching the boy. How is that for hilarious?! The boy was drenched and he left the station running home. He came back with his mother and was she ever furious! The explanation that was given to the mother was "as your son was walking under the opening, a bucket of water was accidently spilled at the second floor opening as your son walked by." I don't think she accepted the story because as she and her son left the station, she said to him, "let's go! These firefighters don't have sense enough to pour piss out of a boot," but I say, that firefighter surely had enough sense to pour water out of a bucket. What an ending!

During my first year as a rookie, one of my two biggest adversaries was a firefighter who from day one made it perfectly clear by his actions that we would never be friends. It was quite obvious to me why. The atmosphere was always tensed and uncomfortable when we were in each others presence. Some years later after I had transferred to another station, advanced in rank, transferred from the fire suppression division into fire administration, and had accepted a divine call from God to preach the gospel of Jesus Christ, we became close friends. In fact, he became one of my two closest friends in the department. Over the years his health began to fail, and I had the opportunity to visit with him in his home as well as the hospital on several occasions. Prior to his death, his wife shared with me that he had asked her to ask me to preach his eulogy at his passing. Before his death, during several conversations between us, he would ask for my forgiveness for his ill treatment of me. Of course I forgave him, and yes, I preached his eulogy at his passing.

Following his funeral that same day, while I was at home, my telephone rang and the caller said, "hello chief, this is (name not mentioned), I just wanted to tell you what a great job you did preaching the funeral today. I also want to tell you how sorry I am for the way we treated you when you worked at the fire station. I apologize not for me alone, but also on behalf of the other firefighters as well. When you were sitting and or kneeling at your bed in the bedroom, reading, studying the Word of God, praying, or just meditating, I remember how we would tease, ridicule you, and talk about you (though not in your presence). The tricks and fun games we played on you never deterred you from your faith in God or your Christian walk. You always treated us with respect although we did not respect you enough to do the same for you. Again, let me say I apologize for our conduct and behavior and ask for your forgiveness. You are truly a man of God and deserved our respect." I extended love and forgiveness and prayed with him before saying goodbye.

There was a second firefighter also, who expressed the same racial bigotry towards me, deeply biased and racially motivated for years after my employment. His deep-seated resentment was quite obvious to me and others in the department. But as they say, "time heals all wounds." Romans 12:10 says, "be kind and compassionate to one another, forgiving each other, just as in Christ, God forgave you."

While sitting at my desk in the Pastors' Study of the church where I pastor, following my retirement, the telephone rang, and this individual said to me that he needed to meet with me at the church, so we could talk. I will admit that I had concerns about this meeting. During the meeting, he stated that he had been teaching a Sunday school class at his church and the subject of the lesson for the up-coming Sunday was on forgiveness, and he could not teach that lesson without asking for my forgiveness. He was obviously led by the Spirit of God to humble himself to ask for my forgiveness. What a cleansing and refreshing of the soul it was for him. This day was the beginning of a brand-new relationship and friendship for each of us.

This firefighter also suffered a decline in his health some years later and I also had the opportunity to visit him during his stay in the hospital as well as in his home for prayer. I will never forget that on one occasion during my hospital visit, as I entered his room, I observed his entire family and many of his relatives were present. To my surprise, he sat up in his bed and in the presence of his family and relatives, he extended his open arms to embrace me. What a powerful display of God's love and forgiveness to us as I expressed my forgiveness to him and prayed for him. Yes, he too became one of my two best friends in the department. I visited with the family during Family Visitation the day of his funeral.

CHAPTER 4

Life in the Community as a Firefighter

I will never forget that one extremely cold winter morning around 2:30 am, with temperatures in the lower teens or less, an alarm was sounded for Command 1, Engine Company 1 (my assigned fire apparatus) and Ladder Truck 1, to respond to a business located adjacent to a "greasy spoon restaurant" two blocks away (another white man's vestige of a private club) for a report of fire. Upon our arrival, it was determined to be a "1071," (a working fire, lay lines). After several hours of fire suppression/extinguishment, and every attempt to control fire spread to the "greasy spoon restaurant," my captain requested that we rotate and take a break and go inside and get some hot coffee. Freezing, we went inside and sat down on the barstools (which I later learned that blacks could not sit, dine, or eat at this eatery). They were only permitted to order to go.

Strangely enough however, management never asked me to get up from the stool and leave the building, but the server served all my fellow firefighter's coffee in porcelain coffee mugs but served me coffee in a throw away styrofoam cup. What did I do? What do you think I did? I will tell you what I did! The weather was too cold for me to allow myself to become *too hot* and turn down a much-needed hot beverage that would warm my extremely cold and nearly frozen body. And besides, I had been chosen to set the standard of respectful, dignified, and intelligent conduct for others that would come after me. What a price we sometimes must pay to receive unbiased and fair treatment in pursuance of equality and justice. That morning and each day after for more than 31+ years, until my retirement, I felt the weight of the world on my shoulders to help achieve racial equality and justice for all mankind. Justice and equality for one should be justice and equality for all.

There were so many fire department activities and functions in the community that revealed or portrayed my life in the community as a firefighter. Herein is just a partial list of those activities. This list is by no means conclusive. These activities took place outside the fire stations and did not occur during actual fire extinguishment, rescue, and fire hazard mitigation. They all are identified under the category of firefighter training.

Periodically, the fire department would acquire abandoned or dilapidated buildings from the city, private citizens, or business owners for live fire training exercises. These buildings would be intentionally set on fire and required a simulated response by fire personnel which in turn required hose lay out, pumper/engine to hydrant connection, and engine set up to supply water to hose lines for fire personnel to extinguish the fire. This scenario was as real as it could get.

Life in the community as a firefighter also required the maintenance of fire hydrants which entailed cutting weeds and bushes from around hydrants, checking for damaged caps and greasing them, replacing gaskets, water flow test, painting, and checking on/off stem for guaranteed proper function.

Let's not forget the periodic testing of hydrants for gallon per minute (GPM) flow to ascertain if hydrants met the required GPM measurements for fire hydrant flow test. This required hose connection to hydrant, engine pumping of water, and the use of a Power Take-off (PTO) gauge in order to ensure accurate GPM measurements for fire hydrant flow test, and that fire hydrants can supply adequate water during an emergency. Pilot gauges made it simple to quickly measure the flow of water from a hydrant and convert readings in pounds per square inch (PSI) to gallons per minute (GPM).

Then there was the water drafting drill. It involved the process of raising water from a static source to supply a pumper. It is known as drafting. This type of operation could be performed from any type of static water source including lakes, ponds, portable tanks, and water carrying vehicles without pumps. This set up would be used when fire hydrants were not available as a water supply.

Fire apparatus driving maneuvers or (apparatus driving operations) were held periodically to ensure that the firefighter would demonstrate a general knowledge of the requirements to drive and operate fire apparatus safely. This training enabled the firefighter to respond more efficiently, thus reducing property damage caused by fires. This was essential in situations where fire damage to the community could be substantial. This training provided me with much needed experience.

Hazmat training or (hazmat awareness and operational training for firefighters) was also a necessity as part of my life in the community as a firefighter. This phase of training allowed firefighters to anticipate potential chemical threats and initiate a safe reaction for civilians and first responders. It also enabled firefighters to respond more efficiently while reducing property damage, health issues, and loss of life.

Vehicular extrication training was conducted regularly at vehicle/automotive junk yards utilizing wrecked vehicles that were used for parts of salvage. Vehicular extrication is the process of removing a vehicle from around a person who has been involved in or trapped in a motor vehicle collision, when conventional means of exit are impossible or unavailable. A delicate approach is needed to minimize injury to the victim during extrication.

Another essential duty of a firefighter is salvage and overhaul training. This also depicted my life in the community as a firefighter. Overhaul in the fire service is the "checking of a fire scene to determine that no fire remains." A close examination ensures that every location where hidden fire could still be burning is searched thoroughly. Salvage is the preservation of the structure and its contents from additional damage resulting from fires, smoke, water, and firefighting activities.

"Overhaul "and "salvage" are distinctly different strategies that require planning for these operations to be successful. The specific needs at an emergency scene will dictate how the strategies will be implemented. An incident may be large enough to require the deployment of numerous units, including the assigning of "salvage groups" or "salvage sectors," or groups small enough to have one or two units accomplish overhaul and salvage simultaneously.

It seems there was no end to the list of duties in my life in the community as a firefighter. So let me close this chapter with the last departmental activity that portrayed my life in the community as a firefighter. This is by no means a complete list of community activities, but hopefully the readers will appreciate the relationship between a firefighter and the community.

I will end with firefighter or fire company building inspections. Firefighter or fire company inspections serve the purpose of allowing firefighters to learn the layout and construction of the buildings, as well as information concerning the products inside, which allows them to work safely during an emergency. In addition, these inspections are for the purpose of the identification of hazards and preplanning to ensure the safety of first responders, improve the safety of the public and occupants, and ensure proper operation of fire alarm and fire suppression systems.

These fire department activities that are conducted in neighborhoods and communities afford an ideal opportunity for readers to relate to life in the community as a firefighter. From the firefighters standpoint, public relations include every contact made with the public as an individual member of the fire service, so planned that the result will be mutually beneficial, through improved fire prevention and fire control.

To sum it all up, regarding life in the community as a firefighter, the readers only need to ask, "why is it important for a firefighter to engage with the community?" When in attendance with the community, firefighters must adapt a sensitive approach to dealing with members of the public and casualties who may be distressed and confused. Firefighters also engage with the community to provide information, advice, and guidance to individuals and groups that focus on health, safety, and wellbeing.

CHAPTER 5

Rookie Mistakes or Just Setup?

If you have never had pranks played on you, just spend some time in a fire station as a firefighter. It seems as if firefighters invented pranks and are the world's greatest pranksters. They just seem to thrive on meeting out the maxim to rookies-always maintaining or ensuring personal safety of course. Pranks were just plain fun, anything for a laugh.

I had only been assigned to Fire Department Headquarters Station for only a few weeks, which seemed like a lifetime or eternity. There was an iron table frame about two feet high and two feet square that needed painting. Being a rookie of course, I was assigned the task of priming the table and another firefighter who had become my friend assisted me. We had completed the job around 10:00 am and around 8:00 pm or 9:00 pm that night, the fire captain told the firefighter who had befriended me to "get your buddy," (me), and the two you clean that lamp black off that table frame. I had unknowingly used what I thought was black primer paint to prime the table but did not know that I was using lamp black instead. Lamp black does not dry unless mixed with paint. My error or (rookie mistake) caused my buddy to suffer the consequences for being my friend. We both had to reprime the table with primer around 10:00 pm that night. Rookie mistake or just plain set-up? You be the judge.

I also experienced an unforgettable and embarrassing situation during my first two weeks on the job. Just before shift break at 7:50 am, I had put away my turnout gear around 7:40 am and was waiting for the shift to end. Suddenly an alarm sounded, and all personnel was dispatched to respond to a "1071" (a working fire, lay lines) at a warehouse building.

Being a rookie, I had unwisely put away my turnout gear before shift change. The other firefighters still had their turnout gear on the fire apparatus, where it should have been until shift break. I should have known not to have removed my turnout gear from the apparatus until after shift break. We were all upstairs in the station when the alarm sounded, and while I was getting into my turnout gear, the firefighters had a head start on me. They slid the pole to board the fire apparatus where their gear was still located. When I had finally finished getting into my gear, and as I ran toward the pole to descend to the fire apparatus floor, they were leaving the station without me. I ran from pole to pole looking down to see what Fire apparatus had not pulled out of the station in order to board whatever fire apparatus possible in order not to miss the fire response.

At the time, I did not know that all I had to do was get a utility vehicle in the station and proceed to the fire response. No one had instructed me to do this in the event this situation or a similar situation would ever occur. Not knowing the procedure, I left the station and headed for home while my crew was actively battling a "1071" (a working fire, lay lines).

The next shift day, my captain asked me where I was during the fire? After I related to him what had occurred, he instructed me what to do in the event this kind of situation or something similar should ever happen again. You may have guessed by now that this was or would have been my first "working fire" since my two weeks on the job. So much for the lack of experience, or experience is the best teacher, we all learn from our mistakes. "Aint that the truth?" Needless to say, that never happened to me again.

CHAPTER **6**

A Candlemakers' Nightmare

It was in the cool of the evening on a summer afternoon and typical of all firefighters, we were sitting outside in front of the downtown fire station (Fire Department Headquarters), when suddenly a man came running from across the street to report a fire on the second floor of a commercial building. He said that two buckets of melted wax were being used for candle making had ignited. Suddenly, all the firefighters (except the Acting Assistant Fire Chief), assigned to the engine company, the ladder company, and the chief's car driver (I mean everyone), left the fire apparatus in the station. We all ran across the street with the idea that we could simply hand carry the buckets of wax out of the building and the incident would be resolved.

As we all entered the building and ascended to the second floor where the candles were being made, we saw the two buckets of burning wax sitting on a table. After a brief discussion and a plan of action was determined, a decision was made to place a broom handle through the handles of the buckets of wax and carry the burning wax down the flight of stairs to the outside. In essence, all we had to do was place a lid over the buckets, starve the burning wax of oxygen, thus smothering the fire, and it would have ended there.

As the Lieutenant from the ladder company picked up the buckets of hot burning wax with the broom handle, and proceeded to the stairwell, and started descending the stairs. He overcompensated thinking that the buckets of wax would slip off the broom handle. He then compensated by raising the broom handle on the end which held the buckets. The buckets of wax slid back down the broom handle towards his body and came to a rest under his unprotected hands and body. His hands were burned so badly that he dropped the buckets into the building's stairwell, and immediately, the entire stairwell erupted in flames, thus trapping all firefighters on the second floor of the building. It was a raging inferno that rendered the stairwell totally inaccessible for the firefighters to exit the building. Now what?!

We all retreated from the stairwell back into the second floor. We had no choice but to run to the windows for a means of escape from the fire. We yelled to the firefighters, who we thought may still be in the station across the street, if any, for help, only to discover that the only firefighter that was not in the station was the Acting Assistant Fire Chief watching the action from across the street in front of the station.

I will never forget what followed. Can you just imagine twelve or thirteen firefighters trapped on the second floor of a burning building by a fire that we caused to spread and block access to the stairwell, while shouting and yelling for help. The Acting Assistant Fire Chief ran back into the station, pulled the station alarm for firefighters to man fire apparatus to respond, only to discover that all the firefighters were in the burning building, and that he was the only one left in the station. After pulling the station alarm what do you think happened next? Nothing! There was no one in the station to respond with the fire apparatus. It was the quick thinking of the Acting Assistant Fire Chief who never entered the burning building, that compelled him to connect several sections of 1½ inch hose to a standpipe in the station, pull it across the street into the building's stairwell and extinguish the fire, thus allowing firefighters to exit the building by way of the stairwell.

The next day, the Roanoke Times and World News featured a story in the headlines titled "A Candlemakers' Nightmare."

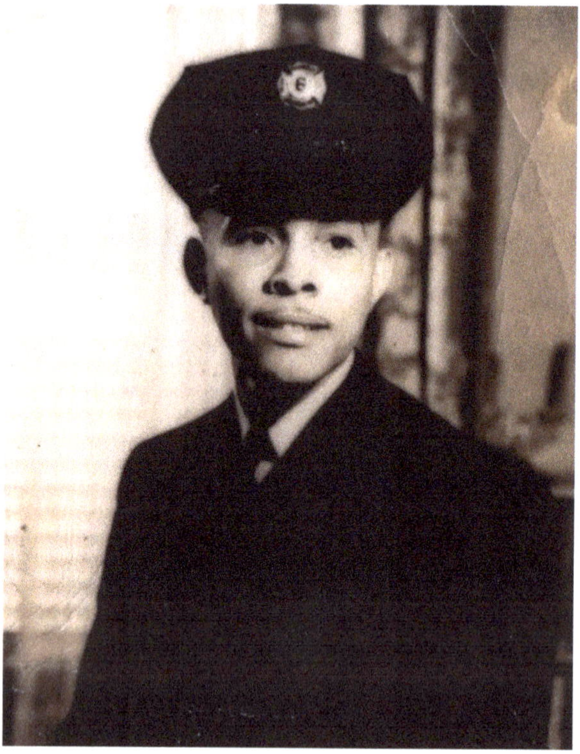

CHAPTER 7

The Lull Before the Storm

Sometimes the not always easily detected practices of racial bias are clearly visible and sometimes they are not. What was clearly a case of racial bias, became obvious and full blown (in your face) type of thing when the "sleeping giant" of racism was awakened as I attempted to progress up the ladder of promotional opportunity and advancement.

The department advertised a vacancy in the Fire Prevention Bureau (later reclassified as the Technical Services Division or the Fire Marshal's Office). This position was classified as a Lieutenant in rank, with the title of Fire Inspector. Another Lieutenant in the department was chosen to fill the position. I did not question his qualifications since he was already a Lieutenant in rank as required by the job description. At the time of the job announcement, I was on the promotional list for Lieutenant, but had not been promoted, therefore I was not eligible for promotion or appointment.

Sometime later (a couple of years maybe), the Fire Prevention Lieutenant became dissatisfied with the Fire Prevention duties and requested to be laterally transferred back into the Fire Suppression Division. Since there was no vacancy in the Fire Suppression Division at the time, his request was denied.

It was at this time that I suggested to Fire Administration that the solution to the dilemma was simple. He wanted out of Fire Prevention into Fire Suppression, and I wanted out of Fire Suppression into Fire prevention. Thereby the dilemma would be resolved. Sounds like a simple fix to a dilemma, doesn't it? Guess again. The official determination from Fire Administration was "Quarles, you have not been promoted to Lieutenant yet and the request cannot be approved." Maybe you have figured out by now the real reason as to why this request was not approved. It was an attempt to maintain an all-white Fire Prevention Division. It's called racial bias, discrimination, and racial bigotry in hiring and promotional opportunities for minorities.

Not until I was officially promoted to the rank of Lieutenant in the Fire Suppression Division sometime later, that we were permitted to transfer to our desired division by means of lateral transfer. I was then a Lieutenant Fire Inspector in the Fire Prevention Division which later became the Fire Marshal's Office. I later became Chief Fire Marshal for the division. How did I become Chief Fire Marshal for the division with the rank of Deputy Fire Chief? Get ready for the fireworks and the answer to this question in Chapter 8.

Match game: New city program teaches fire safety to young arsonists

By GEORGE DYROFF
Staff writer

"You gotta hold the match on its edge," Roanoke Fire Marshal Rawleigh Quarles told the 8-year-old arsonist. "If you hold it flat, it's going to bend, and it will burn your finger."

Why was the city fire marshal teaching this boy, who was charged with murder in a fire that killed an elderly woman, how to light matches?

The instruction was part of the city's new Juvenile Firesetter Counseling and Prevention Program. Open to children under 17, the program is designed to teach fire safety to youngsters who start fires.

The program is a combined effort of the city fire marshal's office, the Roanoke Social Services Department and Mental Health Services of the Roanoke Valley. Roanoke is one of only four Virginia communities that have firesetter prevention projects, and one of 700 across the country.

What more could this child, who was charged Wednesday with setting a Feb. 12 fire in the same block of Patton Avenue Northwest where two years ago he started a fire that killed 73-year-old Kathleen Turner, possibly need to know about matches?

Quite a lot, it turned out. The learning-disabled youth had considerable difficulty lighting paper matches.

The child, whose name has been withheld because of his age, gritted his teeth as he tore a single match from the book. He painstakingly

Please see **Fire**, Page **A-12**

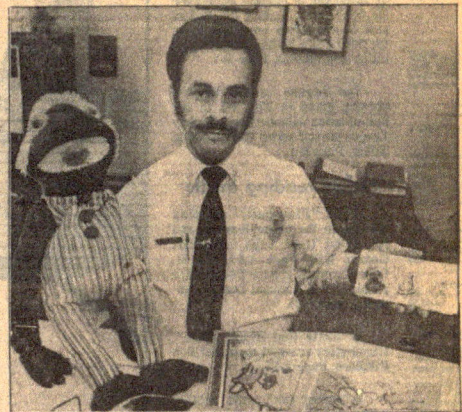

Fire Marshal R.W. Quarles shows toys used in program

Staff photo by WAYNE DEEL

Fire

From Page A-1

closed the cover, as Fire Inspector John Anderson had taught him, and turned the match book over.

The idea of the exercise is to force the child to light so many matches that he gets bored and is no longer fascinated by it.

In his first weekly meeting with Anderson, the boy was asked a series of questions to determine the right counseling. The tests found that this boy — with a smiling, round face and close-cropped hair — needs fire safety instruction and little psychological counseling.

In their second meeting, Anderson, a gentle bear of a man who lavishly praised the boy when he answered correctly, told the story of Snuffy, an animated cartoon fire engine who inspects houses for fire hazards.

During their third class, Anderson quizzed the boy, who knelt on a chair, his elbows on the table, as he eagerly awaited the questions.

"What are some of the bad things he spotted in their homes?" Anderson asked.

"Matches," the child quickly answered and looked to his newfound friend for approval.

"Right-t-t," Anderson smiled and held out his hand so the boy could "give me five."

"If your clothing catches on fire, what should you do?"

"Fall. Stop. Roll," replied the child who wore a long sleeved T-shirt and suspenders to hold up his jeans.

Anderson gently reminded the boy that he would have to stop before he could fall and roll.

Most of the questions gave him little difficulty.

But the matches were another matter. The only way he could light the flimsy paper matches was to hold the head beneath his thumb and draw the match across the striker.

When the match did light, it inevitably burned his finger. He flung it still burning into the ashtray. Spittle flew as he blew out the match and insisted he hadn't been burned.

"Somehow or another you ain't doing something right," Anderson said as he put his arms around the child and tried to take him through the motions.

When asked what good uses matches could be put to, the child remembered that candles, stoves and fireworks could be lit with matches. So could cigarettes and cigars, Anderson suggested.

Yes, but smoking in bed is dangerous, Anderson's apt pupil replied.

The boy's repeated problems with setting fires led Quarles to start a firesetter prevention program, an idea he had for some time.

When the boy was convicted in January of starting a shed fire, the judge, prosecutor and the child's lawyer wondered what could be done to change the youth's behavior. The prevention program was the outgrowth of their concern.

Putting the child in jail doesn't make sense, Quarles said. Unless he receives counseling, he will only repeat his behavior.

Just three weeks after the program began, the parents of four other children have expressed interest in enrolling their kids, Quarles said.

The fire marshal's office has brochures that describe the program and list characteristics of the child arsonist. Behavioral traits include: bed-wetting, playing with matches, cruelty to animals, sexual confusion and aggression. The young arsonist may like to watch fire and is often withdrawn.

Parents who want more information about the program can contact the Fire Marshal's Office, 124 Kirk Ave. S.W. (981-2795).

THE ROANOKE TIMES

City/State

Wednesday, May 5, 1976   15

Roanoke Faces Job Suit Threat

By JOEL TURNER
Times Staff Writer

A report by the U. S. Equal Employment Opportunities Commission (EEOC) has accused Roanoke City of racial discrimination in the case of a black fireman who failed to get a job as a city fire marshal three years ago.

The EEOC has given the city 10 days to say if it is willing to meet with EEOC representatives to resolve the case involving Rawleigh Quarles, a black fire inspector in the city fire department.

Quarles applied for a job as fire marshal three years ago, but the job was given to another man. Quarles filed a complaint with the EEOC, contending that he should have gotten the job because he was the most qualified.

City Manager Byron Haner confirmed Tuesday that the city has received the EEOC report, but he would not discuss it until the report has been given to city council.

Haner said he intends to give the report to councilmen as "expeditiously as possible" because he believes they should consider it.

One source close to council said he believes the city will be willing to meet with EEOC representatives to consider the report.

The EEOC could go to court if it finds the city's response to the report unacceptable, according to one source. It could also take action to get other federal agencies to withhold funds from the city.

Federal law permits funds for the city to be held up if the EEOC isn't satisfied with the city's response to the report.

Haner refused to release a copy of the report, but another source said EEOC investigators have concluded that racial discrimination was involved in Quarles' failure to get the fire marshal's job.

Quarles, who is a lieutenant in the fire department, was a fire inspector when he applied for the fire marshal's job. He is still a fire inspector.

There have been complaints in recent years about racial discrimination in the hiring of city firemen, with the complaints coming mainly from blacks.

There are 12 black firemen among the 215 employes in the fire department.

City officials have maintained the fire department has tried to recruit black firemen.

William Hewitt, director of safety and security, said Tuesday that he couldn't discuss the EEOC report until Haner has taken it to city council.

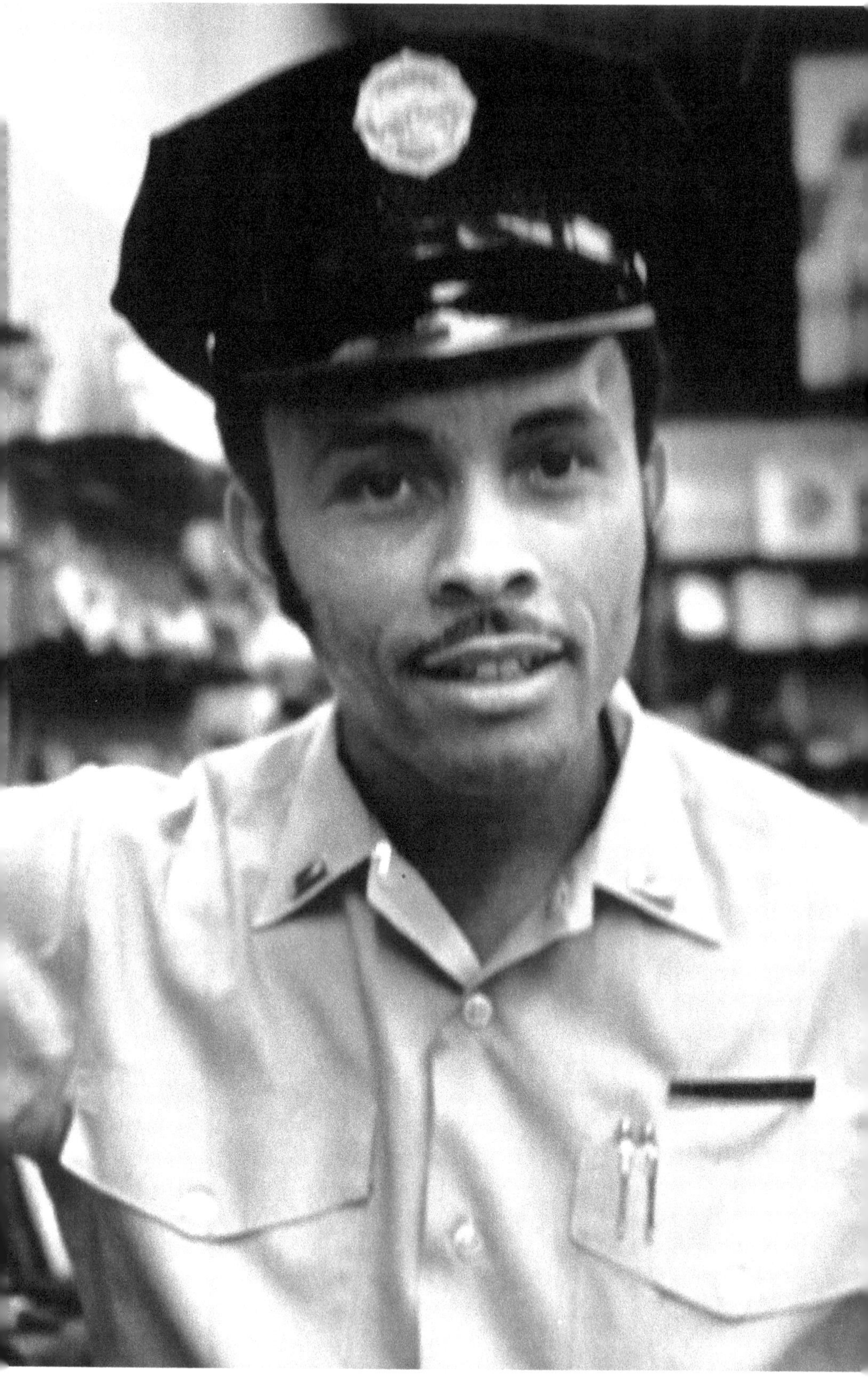

Roanoke Times & World-News

Tuesday Morning, September 13, 1977

Sports
Deaths

Section B

Roanoke Settles Firemen's Bias Case

By JOEL TURNER
Senior Writer

A settlement in a racial discrimination case involving the Roanoke Fire Department will cost the city slightly more than $21,000.

The city has agreed to pay $12,573 in damages and back pay to black firemen to settle the case. The city will also pay another $8,500 in legal fees for attorneys for the black firemen.

As part of the settlement, Rawleigh Quarles, a black fire inspector who failed to get a job as city fire marshal four years ago, has been promoted to fire marshal, effective June 1, 1977.

Quarles, who filed a discrimination complaint against the city after he failed to get the fire marshal's job four years ago, will also receive $5,673 in back pay and will be given seniority as if he had been named a fire marshal on Feb. 1, 1973.

As part of the settlement, a second marshal's job is being created and Quarles has been given the job.

The city has agreed to pay a total of $6,900 in damages to about 25 black firemen as part of the settlement in the separate class discrimination case. Each black fireman will receive several hundred dollars, with the amount based on length of service.

There were two discrimination cases: one involving Quarles' individual promotion, and a second involving discrimination against blacks as a class.

After a closed session Monday night, City Council appropriated the money to settle the case.

Mayor Noel Taylor said council believes the settlement is "fair and equitable" for all parties.

The agreement has been worked out by the city and the black firemen; it has been approved by the U.S. Equal Employment Opportunity Commission (EEOC), which found the city had discriminated against black firemen.

An EEOC report last year concluded the city had discriminated against Quarles as an individual and blacks as a class in hiring and promotion in the fire department.

In settling the class discrimination case, the city has agreed to discontinue the use of the fire department's written examinations unless such examinations have been professionally validated and certified by the EEOC.

The city has also agreed to make "every reasonable effort" to establish and maintain minority representation in the fire department in proportion to the black minority population in the Roanoke area.

There are about 25 black firemen among the fire department's 245 employes, about 10 per cent.

The city has also agreed to notify black applicants who have failed the written tests for the fire department in the past that they can reapply without having to take the written test.

During negotiations to settle the case, Quarles and the black firemen modified the terms of their proposed settlement. Originally, Quarles wanted to be promoted to the next available assistant fire chief's job, and the black firemen wanted monetary relief of $2,000 each per year since 1971.

CHAPTER 8

The Equal Employment Opportunity Commission (EEOC) Determines Roanoke City Fire Department Biased: Quarles Wins Job Discrimination Suit

In 1973, attorneys representing me filed a complaint of racial discrimination and job discrimination with the Equal Employment Opportunity Commission (EEOC), against the City of Roanoke Fire Department. The initial complaint read as follows: "I am a black employee of the City of Roanoke, Virginia. There is a pattern of racial discrimination against black employees at all levels of employment within the city. Blacks are discriminated against in initial employment, promotions, and in other conditions of employment. I was denied a promotion to the position of Fire Marshal because of my race."

I submitted additional proof of my qualifications to the EEOC, which stated that "since none of the other applicants possessed the extensive experience and qualifications that I had acquired as a Fire Inspector, I am convinced that the most qualified applicant was not chosen to fill the position of Fire Marshal, and that I was intentionally, willfully, and systematically discriminated against." I also added a Class Action complaint to the initial complaint.

In addition to being passed over as the most qualified applicant, other tactics were used to disqualify me. The most blatant and obvious tactic used was the re-writing of the job description on several occasions in order to render me ineligible for promotion or appointment. In 1977, 4½ years after filling my initial complaint with the Commission, the City of Roanoke, the EEOC, and the Law Firm of Hill, Tucker, and Marsh of Richmond, Virginia, and I, negotiated an out of court settlement of racial bias with the City of Roanoke Fire Department. Some, but not all of the settlement offer agreed to were as follows:

1. Approximately twenty-two black firefighters in the City of Roanoke Fire Department would receive several hundred dollars each as part of the settlement.
2. The city agreed to stop using entrance examinations for the fire department which the United States Equal Employment Opportunity Commission (EEOC) report determined discriminated against blacks. The black firefighters would receive between $200 and $400 dollars each, depending on their length of service with the department and their rank.
3. The city would agree to create a second Fire Marshal's position and provide about $14,000.00 dollars in back pay and seniority to Rawleigh Quarles.
4. The city would adopt an Affirmative Plan which would govern the hiring and promotional opportunities within all departments in the City of Roanoke.

In August of 1977, the Conciliation Agreement was accepted by all parties and on September 14, 1977, I was appointed Fire Marshal for the City of Roanoke Fire Department.

Let me add that during the period of conciliation, I received hate mail and my children were subjected to harassment in school.

The ROANOKE TRIBUNE

BECAUSE WE LOVE YOU — WE CARE WHAT YOU READ

"The Voice Of The Turtle"

VOLUME XXXVII - NUMBER 18

ROANOKE, VIRGINIA, THURSDAY, SEPTEMBER 15, 1977

Quarles Wins Settlement In Discrimination Suit

RAWLEIGH W. QUARLES

Patience and persistency has finally paid off for Rawleigh Quarles in the descrimination suit filed by him in 1973 against the Roanoke City Fire Department. The 4-year suit has been settled in Quarles' favor indicating that the basic charges brought by him against the City were correct and well-founded.

The settlement will cost the City over $21,000 as Quarles has been awarded over 12,000 in damages and $8,500 for legal fees. In addition the former Fire Inspector has been promoted to Fire Marshall—a position he was denied originally in 1973. Also his seniority will date from that time and he is to receive $5,000 in back pay.

The City has also agreed to pay $8,900 to some 25 Black Firemen who had also filed a Class Action suit for alleged discriminatory practices within the department. Each Fireman will receive several hundred dollars (depending upon the length of service).

Both the Quarles suit and the Class Action suit have been settled fairly, stated Mayor Noel C. Taylor at Monday's Council meeting. Further agreements have been worked out between the City and concerned minority Firemen concerning the employment of minorities. This underscores the fact that the City was guilty of bias in both suits.

The City has further agreed to discontinue the practice of giving written tests for applicants unless such tests have been professionally validated by the EEOC. The Black applicants who have previously failed these tests may now reapply without facing tests.

Fire marshal's suit against city seeks to fill inspector jobs

By JOEL TURNER
Municipal affairs writer

Roanoke Fire Marshal Rawleigh Quarles has sued City Manager Bern Ewert and the city because he has been denied permission to fill two vacant fire inspector jobs.

In the suit, filed in Circuit Court, Quarles contends that as a result of the two vacancies, four fire inspectors are required to carry the workload of six people. This, he said, was hampering the enforcement of fire prevention laws.

In the court papers, the fire marshal argues that Ewert has violated his own policy that allows the filling of vacant jobs that are critical to the community's safety, health and welfare despite city budget problems.

In a policy memorandum last December, Ewert ordered that the filling of non-critical vacant city jobs should be delayed at least two weeks to ensure a balanced budget for the current year. But he said critical jobs affecting the health, safety and welfare of city residents could be filled without administrative delay.

When Quarles was denied permission to fill the vacant fire inspector jobs, he tried to file a grievance over the issue under the city's grievance procedure. But Ewert ruled that Quarles' complaint was not grievable.

In a memorandum to Fire Chief Carl Holt, Ewert said the complaint was not grievable because management has the right to determine the staffing level for fire inspectors as well as the hiring, transfer and assignment of employees.

As a result of Ewert's decision, Quarles filed suit asking the Circuit Court to rule that his complaint is grievable and to order it to be returned to city officials for a full hearing on its merits.

Quarles, who has hired a private attorney to represent him, argues that Ewert has not applied the policy on filling vacancies in a uniform manner.

Nelson Reed, a fire inspector, has joined Quarles as a plaintiff in the suit, which names both Ewert and the city as defendants.

In a copy of the grievance complaint filed with the court papers, Quarles claims that racial and political factors may be involved, but he doesn't mention these issues in the suit.

Quarles, who is black, said his department is the only one in the city that has been ordered to hold open a vacancy indefinitely. He said race may be involved because of his past opposition to racial discrimination in city employment.

As a result of a complaint filed by Quarles several years ago, the U.S. Equal Employment Opportunity Commission found that the city had discriminated against blacks in hiring and promotions in the Fire Department.

Quarles also said Ewert's refusal to allow him to fill the jobs may be politically motivated because Quarles has been a strong advocate of enforcing the fire code.

Quarles is still fighting — but now it's for fire safety

7/82

By ROLAND KIDWELL
Staff writer

Rawleigh Quarles remembers fighting a fire in downtown Roanoke on a frigid day in 1964. A few months earlier he had become one of the city's first two black firemen.

When the blaze was brought under control, the commander suggested that Quarles and the other men visit a nearby greasy spoon for coffee to relieve the numbing chill.

Inside the restaurant, the white firefighters received their coffee in porcelain mugs, those normally reserved for regular customers. Quarles got his in a styrofoam cup.

The young fireman didn't complain. Quarles saved his energy for more important matters.

"There were some times maybe when I had to keep my mouth shut when I didn't want to," Quarles said of his early career as a firefighter, which began in December 1963.

More than nine years later, he complained of discrimination that cost him a promotion. Since winning the job of fire marshal in 1977, Quarles has led a strict enforcement of the city fire code.

Because of these activities, some may view Quarles as a racial agitator or an unbending bureaucrat.

Quarles, 40, said neither description applies. He said he just tries to do what is right, what his Christian values have taught him.

Quarles sports a spit-and-polish look in the blue pants and white shirt of his Fire Department uniform. He is responsible for a bureau that educates the public about fire safety and a staff of six inspectors who probe buildings for fire code violations and investigate suspicious fires.

Rawleigh Quarles
Roanoke fire marshal

Please see **Quarles**, Page **B-9**

THE ROANOKE TIMES, Sunday, May 9, 1976

Roanoke Fire Department Biased, Commission Says

By JOEL TURNER
Times Staff Writer

A report by the U. S. Equal Employment Opportunity Commission (EEOC) says Roanoke City is using entrance tests for its fire department that violate the 1964 Civil Rights Act and discriminate against blacks.

The EEOC report also accuses the city of using promotion policies in the fire department which discriminate against blacks.

The findings are contained in a report dealing with the case of a black fireman who failed to get a job as a city fire marshall three years ago.

The EEOC has concluded there is "reasonable cause" to believe Rawleigh Quarles, a black fire inspector in the fire department, was "discriminated against in promotion because of his race."

A copy of the report was obtained Friday by The Roanoke Times.

Quarles filed a class action complaint on behalf of blacks with the EEOC concerning hiring and promotion policies by the city in the fire department. This complaint was filed in addition to the one dealing with his personal case.

The EEOC report, prepared by Pamela Dillon of the Washington District office of the agency, has concluded the city has discriminated against blacks in both hiring and promotions in the fire department.

City officials have declined to comment on the report except to say they are willing to meet with EEOC representatives to consider it. The EEOC has requested the city and Quarles join with it "in a collective effort toward a just resolution of this matter."

The report says the evidence shows blacks have failed the entrance tests for the fire department at a higher rate than whites, "thus demonstrating a disproportionate impact on black applicants."

The report says data shows in 1974 that 76.9 per cent of the black males and 100 per cent of the black females failed the entrance test for the fire department compared to only 36.2 per cent of the white applicants.

It says that the city hasn't presented any evidence that the test has been "professionally validated," although it involves reading and mechnical skills which it claims are needed in the department.

According to the report, the city has contended that professionally validated tests are even more difficult than the one it gives to applicants for jobs in the department.

The EEOC report says the small percentage of blacks in the fire department (12 out of 212 in August 1974, when the complaint was being investigated) indicates discrimination has taken place.

Blacks constituted 19 per cent of the city's population at that time, but they constituted only 5.6 per cent of the work force in the fire department.

William Hewitt, director of safety and security, said there are now 23 blacks out of 250 employes in the department. The number of firemen was increased as a result of the recent annexation of 16 square miles.

Blacks now constitute about 17 per cent of the city's population.

The EEOC report doesn't deal with conditions in the department since annexation occurred and the additional black firemen have been hired.

It says that certain black employes have been promoted in the fire department, but "it remains that at the time the alleged violations (dealing with Quarles), no black employe had even been promoted above the lieutenant level."

The ROANOKE TRIBUNE, Thursday, May 13, 1976

RAWLEIGH W. QUARLES

Roanoke Fire Dept. Charged With Bias

According to a report just released by the Equal Employment Opportunity Commission, the Roanoke City Fire Department has been weighed and found wanting. After a year of investigation, the EEOC has reported that, "in view of the foregoing evidence, both statistical and otherwise," the Roanoke City Fire Department's "promotion policies have discriminated and continue to discriminate against Black employees as a class in violation of Title VII, as alleged."

The investigation was the result of discrimination allegations filed by Raleigh W. Quarles,, the first Black to be hired by the department (January 1, 1963).

Quarles, presently a Fire Inspector with the department, contends that he was denied promotion due to his race. The EEOC report has confirmed that white firemen less qualified had been promoted to Fire Marshall.

According to the Commission's report, a White witness stated that "the Fire Chief maintained his own clique of associates" among the department personnel and that both of the White selectees considered more competent were "a part of this clique," but that neither appointee had any unusual degree of fire prevention experience outside the routine exposure that Fire Fighters receive."

The investigation further disclosed that the use of statistics is permitted under Title VII to infer a pattern and practice of discrimination and that "no claim or documented evidence was presented that the entrance examinations utilized as part of the hiring process were professionally validated." In 1974, the findings further revealed, 76.9% of the Black males and 100% of the Black female applicants had failed the entrance exams as compared to only 36.2% of the White applicants.

The report stated that "Although certain of the Black employees have been promoted, it remains that at the time of the alleged violations no Black employee had ever been promoted above the Lieutenant Jevel. In addition," it continues, "the evidence shows that the selection authority for appointed positions rests solely with the Chief which authority may serve as a ready mechanism for discrimination."

The Commission and the courts have found that "minority group persons dependent directly upon decisive recommendations from Caucasians cannot expect non discriminatory treatment," the Commission report concluded.

It is reported a Notice of Conciliation Process has been issued by EEOC to both Mr. Quarles and the City in an effort to resolve these serious charges against the Fire Department and its top officials. If this attempt fails Quarles states that he will have no alternative but to go to court.

Roanoke May Create 2nd Fire Marshal Post

By JOEL TURNER
Senior Writer

Roanoke may create a second fire marshal's job in a proposed settlement with a black fire inspector in a racial discrimination case.

Sources said Tuesday the creation of another position is being considered in the settlement with Rawleigh Quarles.

Quarles is a black fire inspector who applied for the job as the city's fire marshal four years ago when it became vacant, but the job was given to R. E. English, who is white.

The U. S. Equal Employment Opportunity Commission (EEOC) concluded in a report more than a year ago that the city discriminated against Quarles by not promoting him to fire marshal.

It couldn't be learned immediately if Quarles would be offered the second fire marshal's job or if the city would seek applications for it.

Sources also said the city has offered Quarles back pay as part of the settlement.

William Hewitt, director of administration and safety for the city, wouldn't confirm the city is considering a second fire marshal's job.

Hewitt said he had no comment on the Quarles case, saying it is being handled by the city's lawyers.

Quarles said Tuesday he had not signed the settlement papers yet and did not want to comment. Quarles filed his complaint with the EEOC in 1973.

The EEOC report concluded that Quarles should have gotten the job because it said he was the most qualified.

The EEOC also concluded that the city had discriminated against blacks as a class in the hiring and promotion practices within the department.

The report said the city has been using entrance examinations for the fire department that discriminate against blacks and violate the 1964 Civil Rights Act.

Quarles demanded that he be promoted to the next available assistant fire chief's position and be given back pay of more than $13,000 as part of the proposed settlement he submitted to the city last year.

Under the EEOC guidelines for settling such cases, the complaining party submits a proposed settlement and the defendant (the City of Roanoke in this case) is given a chance to respond and submit an alternative settlement proposal. The EEOC acts as a mediator in such cases.

Quarles also had proposed that the city discontinue the use of the discriminatory examinations for the fire department and put a freeze on hiring of white firemen.

Black Roanoke fire marshal has had to fight more than fires

By ROLAND KIDWELL
Roanoke Times & World-News

ROANOKE (AP) — Rawleigh Quarles remembers fighting a fire in downtown Roanoke on a frigid day in 1964. A month earlier, he had become one of the city's first two black firefighters.

When the blaze was brought under control, his commander suggested that Quarles and the other men visit a nearby greasy spoon for coffee to relieve the numbing chill.

Inside the restaurant, the white firefighters received their coffee in porcelain mugs normally reserved for regular customers. Quarles got his in a disposable cup.

The young firefighter, now the city's fire marshal, didn't complain and saved his energy for what he said were more important matters.

"There were some times maybe when I had to keep my mouth shut when I didn't want to," Quarles said of his early career.

More than nine years later, Quarles complained of discrimination that cost him a promotion. In 1977, Quarles was winning the job of fire marshal in 1977. Quarles has led a strict enforcement of the city's fire code.

Because of these activities, some view Quarles as an unbending bureaucrat or an agitator. But the 46-year-old Quarles said neither description applies. Quarles is responsible for educating the public about fire safety and supervising a staff of six investigators.

He said he just tries to do what is right — what Christian values have taught him.

Sporting a spit-and-polish look in the blue pants and white shirt of his fire department uniform, Quarles complained that he didn't get the fire marshal's job because he was black and maintained he was more qualified than the white man who got the post.

Four years later, Quarles was promoted to fire marshal and received $14,000 in back pay. Roanoke's other black firemen received a cash settlement after a ruling that they were victims of discrimination.

Another byproduct of Quarles' fight has been a host of complaints from firefighters that the promotion system instituted after Quarles case upset veterans because it disregards seniority.

Some firefighters still resent Quarles, said Duane Dixon, president of the Roanoke Firefighters Association.

But this year, Quarles was battling again, suing the city of Roanoke and asking that a grievance panel hear his complaint that two vacant fire inspector positions should be filled.

He lost the court action but filed a racial discrimination suit against the city — and administrators decided to fill the slots.

Quarles said he doesn't relish complaining and hopes he never has to do it again.

He said he was apprehensive about his first racial discrimination complaint, but afterward he and others found it easier to speak out if they felt they had been wronged.

"I never thought I'd be playing that sort of role, but when I saw my constitutional rights were being violated ... I was going to pursue this matter to its conclusion," Quarles said.

In his first race discrimination complaint, he said, he was shocked by the publicity it engendered.

"It's not my makeup," he said. "It's not my character to be involved in something like this. I'm not a politician. I'm not running for political office."

But Quarles said he'd like to be Roanoke's next fire chief when Fire Chief C.C. Holt retires, perhaps next year.

He said he feels race relations within the department have improved since his two complaints, but

"I'd be less than honest if I didn't say they have a long way to go."

Since boyhood, Quarles wanted to be a firefighter. When he was a boy, however, all firefighters were white. Now 21 of 244 people in the department are black.

That's still far below the city's goal of 18 percent minority hiring in the department — a goal set five years ago.

Quarles said he never thought much about racial discrimination when he was a child, although he noticed the separate water fountains and knew schools were segregated.

He was never subjected to blatant racism until he joined the fire department in 1963, but he tried to be quiet and deal with problems as they arose.

"Integrating a firehouse was a difficult job, he said.

"We lived together as a family 24 hours a day," he said. "We slept in the same bedroom. We ate in the same area, used the same utensils. Naturally, there were some animosities."

Quarles said a few white firefighters went out of their way to help him, but others treated him with indifference. Overt bitterness toward him, however, didn't start until 1973 when he filed his first discrimination complaint.

"What I experienced through this process made my first year in the department seem like an insignificant event," he said. There were harassing phone calls to his wife. His children were confronted by other students at school.

After five years as a fire marshal, Quarles said he believes resentment by other firefighters and citizens has all but disappeared.

"I don't like to think of myself as being the black fire marshal," he said. "I expect to be viewed as the fire marshal who happened to be black."

RAWLEIGH QUARLES EXAMINES FIRE EVIDENCE
Roanoke fire marshal has fought racial discrimination

CHAPTER 9

Fire Code Enforcement and Politics

It did not take long after my appointment to the position of Fire Marshal, that I discovered that there was evidence of weak code enforcement in regards to the use of live Christmas trees and decorative materials in places of assembly and institutional occupancies, including restaurants, overcrowding in places of assembly, sprinkler systems and exhaust systems, automotive paint shops and spray booths, fire lane code enforcement, range hood systems in places of commercial cooking and general fire hazard abatement in businesses, just to name a few.

Strict code enforcement and compliance caused an "awakening of the sleeping giant" and the rearing of the ugly head of politics. Untreated live Christmas trees and flammable decorative materials in certain occupancies were required to be removed and replaced with artificial trees and decorative materials or treated with fire retardant solutions in specific occupancies. Sprinkler systems and exhaust systems were required in automobile spray booths and/or brought into code compliance in existing businesses. Fire lane requirements and strict code enforcement was vigorously enforced. Range hood systems were required or updated to meet code requirements according to the fire code. Last, but not least, code violations and fire hazards were required to be abated in a specific time. Failure to do so resulted in court action, or other means to assure compliance.

For failure to comply, businesses where extreme hazards and potential explosions existed were closed, and pad locked by the Fire Marshal's Office. Business owners were summoned to court before a judge by the Fire Marshal's Office and fined for failure to comply. As a result of this strict and aggressive code enforcement, business owners began complaining to members of city council. On one occasion, I had to go to the mayor for his intervention to members of city council to require the city manager to fill two vacancies in the Fire Marshal's office which had existed for some time. A memo from the City Manager's Office read "vacancies of non-essential personnel will not be filled due to budget constraints," but I knew the real reason. It was politics and personal issues between me and the city manager that caused the rift. The issue was resolved, and the vacancies were filled immediately after members of council agreed with me that the positions were essential to ensure life safety, fire safety, and fire prevention. So much for me and the city managers relationship. After that contest, and oh, I forgot to mention that I filled a greivence against the city manager which caused members of council to intervene. The Circuit Court had already ruled in favor of the city manager, but members of council ruled in my favor and brought about a resolution to the issue. I must clarify however, that this was not the same city manager that selected and appointed me to the position of fire chief.

Because of strict adherence to fire code enforcement and scientific arson investigations citywide, accidental and or intentional fire loss decreased. In addition, life loss, injury, property loss and damage were decreased in the City of Roanoke.

Quarles

FROM PAGE A1

ment skills needed for the top job, Snead said.

Quarles has attended many seminars to improve his management skills, Snead said. "He has long held the goal of being chief and he has worked towards that for many years."

Quarles said today that he hopes to improve the professionalism and pride in the Fire Department.

"My desire is to effectively and efficiently lead the city's Fire Department. I hope to help enhance the professionalism, pride, enthusiasm and leadership qualities of the members of the organization as we work together to provide the highest level of fire protection for citizens and property," Quarles said.

Quarles clashed with city administrators over issues of racial discrimination in the early 1970s, but that wasn't mentioned by Herbert's statement announcing his appointment. The controversy occurred before Herbert began working for the city.

Almost 10 years after joining the Fire Department, Quarles complained that he didn't get the fire marshal's job because he was black. He maintained that he was more qualified than the white man who got the job. He filed a complaint with the federal Equal Employment Opportunity Commission.

The federal agency ruled that the city had discriminated against Quarles and other black firefighters. The result was that Quarles was promoted to fire marshal in 1977 and given $14,000 in back pay. Roanoke's other black firefighters received a cash settlement from the city after the ruling that they were discrimination victims.

But Quarles said that he has never considered himself to be an agitator despite his clash with city officials.

"I never thought I'd be playing that sort of role, but when I saw my constitutional rights were being violated ... I was going to pursue this matter to its conclusion," Quarles said in an interview several years ago.

Quarles also battled with city administrators again in 1982 when he sued the city and asked that a grievance panel hear his complaint that two vacant fire inspector jobs be filled. Administrators decided to fill the open slots while the grievance was pending.

Quarles is a graduate of the former Lucy Addison High School and has taken courses in fire science at Virginia Western Community College and the National Fire Academy in Emmitsburg, Md. He has been certified by the state as a fire inspector III and fire/arson investigator III, the highest attainable level. In addition, he is certified as an adjunct fire instructor.

Quarles is a member of the Building Officials and Code Administrators International, the International Association of Arson Investigators and the NAACP. He is married to the former Barbara Ann Girst, and the couple has one daughter, Nicole, 14, and two sons, Rawleigh Jr., 24, and Derrick, 19.

Quarles, who was then a fire inspector, was not used to the publicity. He said he was "shocked when I was thrust into that situation. It's not my make-up. It's not my character to be involved in something like this. I'm not a politician. I'm not running for political office."

Others in the department believe he is running to succeed Fire Chief C.C. Holt when Holt retires, perhaps next year. Quarles says he'd like to be Roanoke's fire chief. Dixon and other firemen have similar ambitions.

Racial relations since Quarles' complaint was settled have improved in the department, he said, but "I'd be less than honest if I didn't say they have a long way to go."

As a child, Quarles decided he wanted to be a fireman. When he discovered in 1963 that the city was seeking minority applicants he was one of the first to apply.

Quarles recalled fire engines answering calls in front of his Rutherford Avenue home where he moved with his family when he was 7. He said he admired the equipment and the excitement generated when the fire trucks arrived.

Back then, of course, all the firemen were white. Now, 21 of 244 people in the department are black, well below the 18 percent goal for minority hiring set when Quarles' complaint was settled five years ago.

When he and Joe Crutchfield became the first blacks in the Roanoke Fire Department in 1963, they were warned by then-Fire Chief Sidney Vaughan that they would "hear things you don't want to hear" such as racial slurs.

While growing up, Quarles had noticed "white" and "colored" water fountains and segregated schools, but he said he had never been blatantly subjected to racism until he joined the department.

7/3/82

EDITORIALS / LETTERS

After all, better service

ROANOKE officials have decided to fill two vacant fire inspector positions, and Fire Marshal Rawleigh Quarles has dropped his racial discrimination complaint against the city. Nice ending all around.

But the issue, which had all of the earmarks of a minor power play, probably should not have had the racial element dragged in. Quarles, who is black, has had disagreements with the city manager's office over duties and procedures. But the high performance in his office has never been questioned, particularly in the field of arson investigation, perhaps the fastest-growing need in the city.

Whatever the disagreement between the fire marshal and the city, the city appeared to be holding the positions, the money for which is in the budget, as "hostages." Quarles countered: first with a complaint about the open positions, a complaint the city said did not fall within the regular grievance procedure; then with a suit to force a hearing of the complaint; then — after a negative court ruling — with a racial discrimination complaint that would fall under the grievance procedure.

Quarles perhaps overreacted in labeling the disagreement racial, but he succeeded in getting the attention of city officials, primarily because he took the discrimination-complaint route once before, with success.

In retrospect, the discrimination complaint may have been the only way he had to force the city's hand.

The middle man in the happy tale — happy, because the need for two additional fire inspectors has been amply shown — was Councilman James Trout, who persuaded city officials to advertise the two openings.

Trout saw the need and acted, putting aside all the extraneous issues and concentrating on the central issue: more arson requiring a higher level of inspection.

City manager upheld in fire jobs dispute

By JOEL TURNER
Municipal affairs writer

A Roanoke Circuit Court judge has upheld a decision by City Manager Bern Ewert in a dispute over filling two vacant fire inspector jobs.

Judge Kenneth Trabue ruled that Ewert and management have the right to determine whether vacant fire inspector jobs will be filled.

He affirmed Ewert's decision that a complaint by Fire Marshal Rawleigh Quarles over the issue is not grievable.

Quarles, who was denied permission earlier this year to fill two vacant inspector jobs, tried to file a grievance over the issue under the city's grievance procedure.

Ewert ruled that Quarles' complaint was not grievable because management has the right to determine staffing levels as well as the hiring, transfer and assignment of employees.

In the suit, Quarles asked the court to rule that his complaint was grievable and to order it to be returned to city officials for a hearing on its merits.

Please see **Ewert**, Page **A-6**

Ewert

From Page A-3

But Trabue, in a letter to attorneys in the case, said, "It appears to me to be overwhelmingly clear that the filling of vacancies for fire inspectors ... is a responsibility exclusively reserved by management, which has the right to manage the affairs and operation of the city ... and that the complaints of the plaintiffs are non-grievable ..."

Nelson Reed, a fire inspector, joined Quarles as a plaintiff in the suit, which named both Ewert and the city as defendants.

In a policy memorandum last December, Ewert ordered that the filling of non-critical vacant city jobs should be delayed at least two weeks to assure a balanced budget for the current year. But he said critical jobs affecting the health, safety and welfare of city residents could be filled without administrative delay.

In the suit, Quarles, who hired a private attorney to represent him, contended that the inspector jobs are critical to city safety. As a result of the vacancies, he said, four inspectors are required to carry the workload of six people. This, he said, is hampering the enforcement of fire prevention laws.

Quarles said his department was the only one that had been ordered to hold open a vacancy indefinitely.

Ewert said earlier the city was making a study of the staffing level for fire inspectors. He said the filling of the inspector jobs was being held up in the meantime.

In a copy of the grievance complaint filed with the court papers, Quarles, who is black, claimed that racial and political factors may have been involved in the case, but he didn't mention those issues in the suit.

As a result of a complaint filed by Quarles several years ago, the U.S. Equal Employment Opportunity Commission found that the city had discriminated against blacks in hiring and promotions in the Fire Department.

Roanoke fire marshal drops racial-discrimination complaint

By ROLAND KIDWELL
Staff writer

Roanoke Fire Marshal Rawleigh Quarles said Tuesday night that he was dropping a racial discrimination complaint against the city because Roanoke officials have decided to fill two vacant fire inspector positions.

Councilman James Trout said he had asked the city administration to fill the posts two weeks ago because the additional employees were necessary for effective fire prevention and arson investigation.

Quarles' complaint had reached City Manager Bern Ewert and would have gone next to a city grievance panel. But Robert Herbert, assistant city manager, said the city had authorized advertising the two openings.

Herbert said a study of city inspection departments found that the two positions needed to be filled to maintain the current level of fire protection services. "We had no reason to hold (the jobs) open," he said.

Trout revealed Tuesday night that he had asked the city administration in a closed session two weeks ago to fill the fire inspector posts.

"Roanoke's fire prevention bureau is one of the tops in the state. The conviction rate is astronomical in arson cases," Trout said. With the two open positions, he said, the four inspectors were doing the work of six employees.

"The men couldn't get vacations," he said. Trout said they often were called in the middle of the night to investigate suspicious fires, which is a big help to the police.

Because the number of inspectors will return to its past level, "I have no reason to pursue the grievance issue ... I'm elated that the positions are being filled," Quarles said.

Quarles filed suit against the city in February to get his complaint heard after Ewert said Quarles' original complaint over the job vacancies did not fall under the city grievance procedure.

Judge Kenneth Trabue ruled that Ewert and city management had the right to determine whether the vacant fire inspector jobs would be filled. Quarles, who is black, then pursued a racial discrimination complaint through the city grievance procedure.

That complaint was pending when the city decided to fill the two inspectors' positions.

In a copy of the grievance complaint filed in the winter with cou... Quarles had claimed that racial cal factors may have been invol... case. Quarles said his strong enfo... the fire code could have caused th... to remain vacant.

Asked Tuesday if he believed crimination was involved in k... positions unfilled, Quarles said, "... position is the same ... I don't w... it up again."

As the result of a complai... Quarles several years ago, the Employment Opportunity Co... found that the city had disc... against blacks in hiring and pro... the Fire Department.

Ewert had said earlier that the city was studying the staffing level for fire inspectors. He said filling the inspectors' jobs was being delayed in the meantime.

In a policy memo last December, Ewert ordered that the filling of non-critical vacant city jobs should be delayed at least two weeks to ensure a balanced budget. But he said critical jobs affecting the health, safety and welfare of city residents could be filled without administrative delay.

Quarles said the vacancies hampered the enforcement of fire prevention laws and thus were detrimental to the welfare of city residents.

169 want to be fire chief

By JOEL TURNER
MUNICIPAL WRITER

Roanoke has received 169 applications from across the country for the fire chief's job.

George Snead, director of administration and public safety for the city, said he hopes a new chief can be named by late June or early July.

"We are going to do it as soon as possible," Snead said.

The city advertised the job in national publications as well as locally.

"We've got applications from the Midwest, North and other areas, although the majority have come from Virginia and the Middle Atlantic States," Snead said.

It is the third time in the past six years that the city has conducted a search for a new fire chief.

Harry McKinney, a 36-year veteran of the Fire Department, retired for health reasons last December after serving as chief for less than two years. McKinney succeeded Jerry Kerley, who resigned under pressure in the summer of 1987 during a controversy about his personal life.

City officials plan to appoint a panel to interview and screen the finalists, similar to the procedure used in the past to select a fire chief, Snead said.

The city's two senior deputy fire chiefs, Billy Akers, deputy for administration, and Rawleigh Quarles, deputy for training, have served as acting chiefs since McKinney retired.

Snead said the plan for Akers and Quarles to each serve as acting chief for about three months was discussed with them. Akers served as acting chief the first three months after McKinney retired, and Quarles has been acting chief since then.

"We have two senior deputy chiefs and we thought this arrangement would give both a chance to have experience as acting chief," Snead said.

Akers and Quarles are thought to be top contenders for the job.

When McKinney retired, Snead said the city would have open competition for the chief's job and wouldn't restrict it to applicants from within the Fire Department.

When Kerley was hired in 1983, there was controversy because he didn't come from within the ranks. Kerley had been fire chief in Albemarle, N.C. Six of the 12 finalists for the job then came from within the department.

The Roanoke Fire Fighters Association, the firefighters' union, and several City Council members said that they thought the new chief should have come from within the ranks.

CHAPTER 10

Arbitrarily Transferred from the Fire Marshal's Office

By now, everyone (business owners, property owners, politicians, city officials, city manager, members of city council, and contractors), were beginning to feel the effect of strict code enforcement. As a result, the Fire Marshal's office was beginning to experience political pressure. However, the Fire Marshal's office was not deterred, in fact, we became more determined and resolute in the execution of our sworn responsibility to enforce the fire code for the protection of life and property for the residents of the City of Roanoke from fire, loss of life, injury from fire, and damage to property.

At this time in my career, I was still considering my careers ambition and goal with a determination to climb the ladder of success and reach my journey to the top. I must ask in all earnestness and sincerity, what other pitfalls would be placed in my pathway as stumbling blocks, obstacles, and deterrences to prevent me from reaching my goal, or my journey to the top.

I was blindsided and did not see this coming. In 1987, I was arbitrarily (without my consent), transferred from the position of Chief Fire Marshal in the Fire Marshal's office (Deputy Chief of Technical

Services) to the Training and Safety Division as Deputy Chief for Training and Safety. I call to your attention the Conciliation Agreement and Consent Decree of 1977, which required my appointment to the position of Chief Fire Marshal/Deputy Chief of Technical Services Division.

Neither of the other three Deputy Chiefs wanted the position of Training and Safety Division, and neither did I. It did not take a rocket scientist to see that this was a systematic effort to remove me from the position of Deputy Fire Chief for Technical Services Division/Chief Fire Marshal. The games people play as I stated, I was blindsided and did not see this coming.

So, what did I do?! Here's what I did. I strongly protested this administrative decision by reminding all parties involved in the out of court settlement that this action was in strict violation of the consent decree with the EEOC. The consent decree included the following as it pertained to my part of the accepted settlement:

1. Charging party Quarles shall be promoted to Fire Marshal effective June 1, 1977.
2. Charging party Quarles shall be paid as back wages the sum of $14,000.00.
3. Charging party Quarles shall be accorded seniority, as if he had been promoted to the job of Fire Marshal on February 1, 1973.

The other three major sections of the consent decree included hiring policies, promotional policies, and class relief, which included a total of eight subcategories that are not detailed in the book.

I immediately reminded the Fire Chief, Director of Safety and Security, members of city council, and the mayor, that any attempt to arbitrarily remove me from the Fire Marshals position without my consent would constitute a blatant violation of the consent decree and would land the city into a court of law. Guess what? They all agreed and did not pursue that reckless plan of action. Who's keeping score of wins and losses?

Later, however, I was introduced to a new plan of action (not forced), that would only be pursued with my consent. The city manager met with me in his office (at his request) and asked me if I would consider the transfer on an interim basis for a period of ninety days in which to see if this new assignment/transfer (if I accepted), would be a positive career move for me. It was also stated by the city manager that if I was not satisfied with my new assignment, after a reasonable period of time (ninety days), that upon my request, I would be reassigned or transferred back to the Technical Services Division and resume my duties as Deputy Chief/Chief Fire Marshal.

Well, are you ready for this? Are you really ready for this?! I mean really, really, ready for this?!! After a period of ninety days, serving as Deputy Fire Chief for the Training and Safety Division, I decided to remain in my new position. It was really a challenge and an inspiration, and a test of my ability and management skills, not to mention my leadership skills.

I remained in this position from 1987 to 1989. During such time, I was given the opportunity to serve as Acting Fire Chief from March of 1989 to July 1989. The Fire Chief had retired, and a new Fire Chief had not been named during that time. Well as God would have it, in July 1989, I was appointed to the position of Fire Chief for the City of Roanoke by the Roanoke City Manager.

After serving as Fire Chief for almost four years, in 1992, one day just after I had arrived home from the office, my telephone rang, and it was the Director of Administration and Public Safety. He asked me to come to his office. He also stated that members of the Virginia State

Police had launched an investigation of me concerning allegations of the misuse of state funds, rigged bids on fire trucks, and the acceptance of improper gratuities from a fire equipment manufacturer (none of which were true) as the investigation later revealed.

This investigation was initiated by a group of firefighters who had sent a letter to the State Attorney General listing the allegations against me. The State Attorney General then directed the Virginia State Police to conduct the investigation. The State Police spent three months investigating the complaint alleged against me, but no charges were filed. Roanoke's Commonwealth's Attorney said, "there was no evidence to support criminal charges." A news story in the Roanoke Times and World News (Virginia Section), dated March 1, 1993, said "some of his own men made the allegations that led to a State Police probe, which eventually exonerated him."

Again, I ask you, are you keeping score of wins and losses?

My goal to climb the ladder of success and my quest to reach the top had finally been achieved which had consumed 31+ plus years of my career. The last 5½ years, I served as Fire Chief, totaling 31+ years and three months.

I say to God be the glory! If it had not been for the Lord who was on my side! I owe Him all the praise, glory, and honor, for it was only possible because of His favor, blessings, and mercy in my life. For without Him, none of this would have been possibly achieved. I thank Him for the blessing of the job, His guidance, direction, and protection, His ability, and His divine favor and love for me through it all.

After serving for 5½ years as Fire Chief, it became apparent that God's divine plan for my life included a "higher calling" than that of Fire Chief.

Quarles

FROM PAGE C1

four years, said the investigation was unpleasant for him and his family. After it was over, Quarles said, he just wanted to get back to managing the Fire Department.

Since then, the tension that developed in the department after the state police probe became public has eased. As far as Quarles is concerned, the incident is over.

"I've got too many important

RAWLEIGH QUARLES
ROANOKE FIRE CHIEF

- **Age:** 51.
- **Hometown:** Roanoke.
- **Education:** Lucy Addison High School; fire control and prevention courses at Virginia Western Community College, College of William and Mary, the National Fire Academy and other schools.
- **Professional:** Joined the Roanoke Fire Department as a firefighter in 1963. In the past 30 years, has held several positions, including fire inspector, fire marshal, head of the Fire Prevention Bureau and deputy chief for training and safety. Appointed chief in 1989.
- **Family:** Married with three children.
- **Quote:** "We are busy. A lot is going on. Some days, there are not enough hours or people to accomplish as much as we would like."

Fire department program improves response times

By JOEL TURNER
STAFF WRITER

Roanoke's first-responder program, in which firefighters trained as emergency-medical technicians respond to calls until paramedics arrive, has been operating at three stations for two years.

The program recently was instituted at Station No. 13 in the Peters Creek area. It is to be expanded next year to include Station No. 10 near the airport.

The first-responder program is similar to a system that is operating at Station No. 4 in Southwest Roanoke, No. 11 in Southeast and No. 14 in Northeast off Orange Avenue.

The response times in the Peters Creek and upper Northwest community averaged 8.2 minutes in the past year — slower than the goal of 6 minutes that is considered critical in life-threatening emergencies. For the city as a whole, the average response time on emergency-medical calls was 5.2 minutes in 1992, down from 6.2 minutes in 1991.

Response times have been reduced by an average of 3 minutes in the areas where the first-responder program is operating.

The city has a combined Emergency Medical Services system that includes three groups: full-time paramedics, firefighters at four fire stations and volunteer rescue squad members.

Until the city switched to a combined system five years ago, the volunteers operated as the Roanoke and Williamson Road lifesaving crews.

The squads were consolidated into the Roanoke Emergency Medical System Inc., which has 120 volunteers to help provide the service. The city has 25 full-time and 26 part-time emergency-medical employees. About half of the city's 244 firefighters have received EMS training.

Fire Chief Rawleigh Quarles said he hopes that eventually all firefighters will be trained as EMS technicians. That would enable the city to establish a first-responder program at all fire stations or merge the EMS system with the Fire Department.

Nationwide, there is a trend toward merging EMS programs with fire departments.

Quarles said he thinks the city's combined system is operating smoothly, although a merged system might be more efficient. He denied an allegation made by some volunteers that the Fire Department is trying to take over the EMS system and force the volunteers out.

City Council voted recently to continue the combined system for at least one more year.

Councilman William White said he believes the city could answer emergency calls faster and save money if its EMS system were merged with the Fire Department. The volunteers still would be needed in a merged system, he said. But some volunteers don't like the idea of merger.

"It would be the end of the volunteers," said Sidney Robertson, president of the Roanoke Emergency Medical Services Inc.

City Manager Bob Herbert has assured council that the volunteers are needed to work with the city's paid EMS workers and firefighters in the combined system.

Before 1985, the city relied exclusively on volunteer lifesaving crews, in keeping with its heritage as the home of the first volunteer rescue squad in the world.

But the city began hiring full-time paramedics and emergency-medical technicians when emergency calls began increasing rapidly and membership in the volunteer lifesaving crews dwindled.

Because of decreasing membership, the volunteer crews did not have enough staff to answer medical calls during the day. The number of paid emergency personnel has gradually increased in recent years.

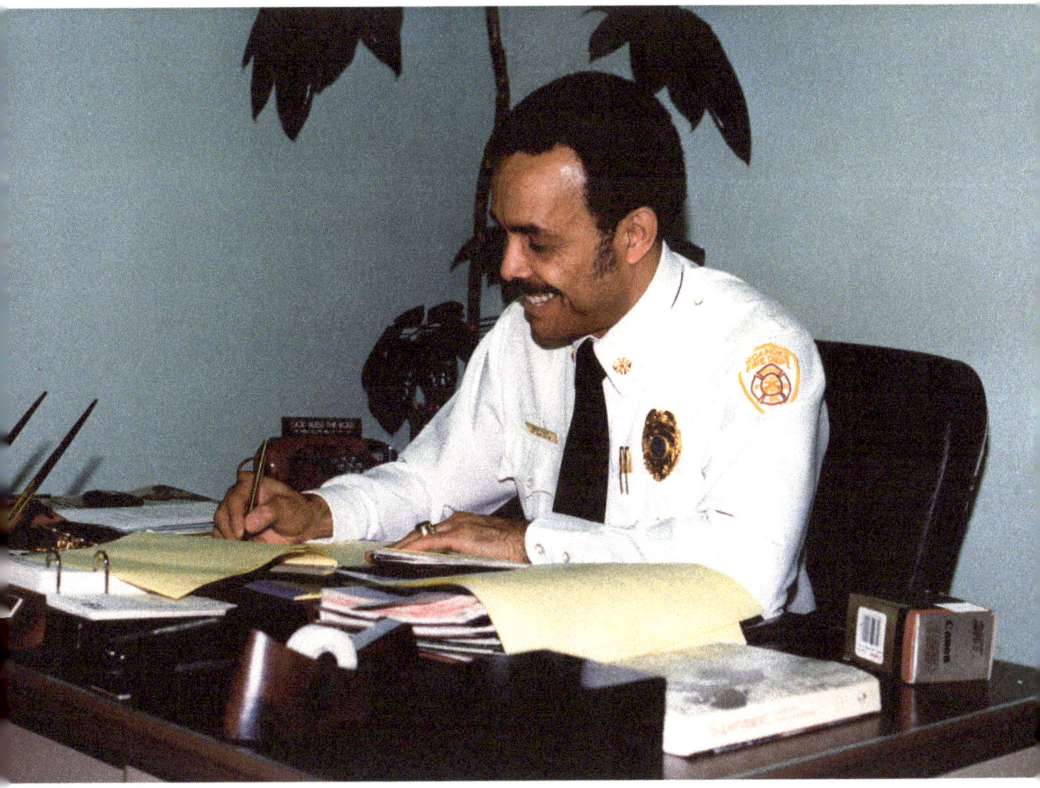

7.16.87

Roanoke fire official reported unhappy about reassignment

By JOEL TURNER
Municipal writer

Rawleigh Quarles, Roanoke's deputy fire chief for technical services and the highest-ranking black in the Fire Department, has been reassigned as part of a reshuffling of the department's top management.

Quarles has been named deputy chief for training and safety.

Quarles has served as deputy chief for technical services since 1985, when he was promoted in a reorganization of the department.

As a deputy chief, he also has remained city fire marshal, a job he has held since 1977.

But Quarles has been given new duties and will no longer be fire marshal.

Quarles is reportedly upset by the move and has hinted to at least one firefighter that he may contest it.

Quarles wouldn't comment on the situation Wednesday, but he has retained an attorney.

"It is in the hands of my attorney and I'm reserving comment on it now," he said.

Fire Chief Jerry Kerley couldn't be reached for comment on Quarles' new assignment, which took effect this week.

But Kerley's immediate supervisor said Quarles was reassigned because officials think he is the best man to oversee training for the department.

"You fit the talents of your personnel to the current needs of the department," said George Snead, director of administration and safety.

"Simply stated, we need his talents for this job," Snead said. "This is no demotion. We think Rawleigh can do a good job for us in this assignment."

Quarles is being shifted to a job that is equal in pay and rank to his current position, said City Manager Robert Herbert.

Please see **Fire official**, Page **A16**

Rawleigh Quarles
Will no longer be fire marshal

Fire official

From Page A1

Herbert said he considered Quarles' new job to be a "positive" move that could better prepare him for possible future promotions.

Without commenting specifically on Quarles, Herbert said the city's management approach is to give "supervisory people as wide experience as possible so they work in a number of areas so they can position themselves to compete successfully in the future for higher management jobs."

Quarles has done a good job as fire marshal and deputy chief for technical services, Herbert said. There is nothing negative about the reassignment, which was part of the plan to combine four deputy chief jobs into three, he said.

The changes leading to Quarles' reassignment were triggered by the recent retirement of Paul Webb, deputy chief for operations.

Deputy Chief Harry McKinney, who had supervised training and safety for the department, has been named to fill Webb's job. Quarles has taken over McKinney's old job and Deputy Chief Billy Akers has taken over Quarles' job.

Akers, in addition to becoming fire marshal and deputy chief for technical services, will continue to oversee administration.

Since the positions of deputy chief were established in 1985, Snead said, it had been the city's intention to consolidate the four posts into three when someone retired.

Snead said the deputy chiefs were consulted before the reassignment of duties, but he wouldn't say whether they were given the chance to veto it.

The reshuffling of duties "wasn't done with regard to an individual in mind. This was done with regard to the three deputy chiefs' positions and what is in the best interests of the Fire Department," Herbert said.

"This is a story about the reassignment of three people. I consider it positive for all three," Herbert said, "because it will expose them to new management responsibilities."

Unless the city provides a chance for current employees to get wide experience, he said, "the accusation can always be that you've kept me in one position and never given me the opportunity to cross over and work in other areas."

Herbert said the three deputy fire chiefs' jobs are "of equal status, pay and rank. There is not a first among equals in those three positions. There is no senior, middle or junior deputy fire chief."

Quarles, 45, has worked for the city since December 1963. He was one of the city's first two black firefighters.

He won the fire marshal's job in the settlement of a racial discrimination case. Ten years after joining the department, he complained that he didn't get the fire marshal's job because he was black. He maintained he was more qualified than the white man who got the post.

Quarles was promoted to fire marshal and given back pay when the discrimination case was settled in 1977.

The city's other black firefighters received a cash settlement from the city after a ruling that they were discrimination victims.

Quarles was promoted to deputy chief for technical services two years ago, but he retained the fire marshal's job because it was part of the technical services division.

EDITORIALS

One bad hand dealt in reshuffling

THE REASSIGNMENT of Rawleigh Quarles to new duties in the Roanoke Fire Department is not a demotion, city officials are quick to point out. Maybe not, but the treatment he's receiving does appear to be a slight.

Quarles, the highest-ranking black in the city Fire Department, will receive the same pay as in his old job but isn't happy with his assignment as deputy chief for training and safety. By all accounts, he did well as deputy fire chief for technical services and fire marshal. At the very least, an employee who does his work satisfactorily normally gets to keep his job. Not so with Quarles.

Duties of all three deputy chiefs are changing following the retirement of the fourth, Paul Webb, deputy chief for operations. Part of the reason for that is that the four jobs will be consolidated into three.

All three of the deputies had sought Webb's job, which oversees the daily firefighting operation. In the reshuffling, there seems to be added responsibility for everyone but Quarles. Webb's job is going to Harry McKinney, the current deputy for training and safety. The other deputy chief, Billy Akers, will take over Quarles' old duties plus continue to oversee administration.

Fire Chief Jerry Kerley says Quarles was reassigned because he thought Quarles' skills were needed in the training division. City Manager Robert Herbert said he believes Quarles' new job to be a positive move that could better prepare him for future promotions. Without commenting directly on Quarles' future, Herbert said the city's management approach is to give supervisors "as wide experience as possible ... so they can position themselves to compete successfully in the future for higher management jobs."

There's nothing wrong with that philosophy, but at the same time an employee who is viewed as top-management material ought to have a challenging post in the interim. The job of deputy chief for training and safety will give Quarles more contact with the department's firefighters than he has now. That could help to build rapport with new people, which would be useful down the line to someone in, say, the fire chief's job. But in the meantime, Quarles will have less direct supervisory responsibility than in his old job.

Roanoke City Council is powerless to act on Quarles' behalf, because the city charter prevents elected officials from interfering with decisions involving personnel who do not report directly to them. That is a sound principle; day-to-day operation of the city administration should be removed from politics.

At the same time, council members ought to have some recourse when they receive complaints from citizens about a personnel decision, such as the Quarles case. Mayor Noel Taylor may have found an acceptable way to influence this matter with his public suggestion that City Manager Robert Herbert meet with Quarles to try to appease him. Herbert has ultimate responsibility for city personnel decisions.

Quarles no doubt would develop some new skills in the job of directing training for firefighters, and he ought to be willing to give that a try. However, a good manager doesn't strip a valued employee of his responsibilities against his will in order to teach him a new skill.

Quarles isn't likely to go into this new job without a fight. After all, he had to fight to get where he is now in the department. He won the fire marshal's job in the settlement of a racial discrimination case.

The city doesn't need the kind of bad publicity that another discrimination suit would bring. Herbert has an opportunity to douse this smoldering fire by drawing up a job description for Quarles giving him duties that at least are equal to those of his old post.

Roanoke planning national search for new fire chief

Local contenders expected for post

By JOEL TURNER
Municipal writer

Roanoke will make a national search for a new fire chief, but there are likely to be strong local contenders for the job.

When Jerry Kerley was hired four years ago, six of the 12 applicants who were interviewed for the job came from within the city Fire Department.

The city's deputy fire chiefs and others in the department are potential candidates for the chief's job, just as they were in 1983 when Kerley was hired.

All of the deputy chiefs — Harry McKinney, Rawleigh Quarles and Billy Akers — are veteran firefighters who are familiar with the city and the department.

City Manager Robert Herbert denied that the decision to make Kerley's resignation public and have him step down as chief Friday was related to the controversy surrounding the recent reassignment of Quarles.

Herbert said that has been resolved. He said Quarles has agreed to accept his new assignment as deputy chief for training and safety.

Kerley, the first fire chief from outside the local ranks, resigned Friday, less than four years after he took the job.

Herbert said that he and Kerley "mutually agreed" that it would be best for him to quit because publicity about his personal life had diminished his effectiveness as chief.

Some firefighters had complained about his management style, that there was favoritism in promotions, that he increased the bureaucracy in the department and reduced the manpower for fighting fires.

When Kerley was hired by former city manager Bern Ewert, a majority of council and the Roanoke Fire Fighters Association wanted someone within the deparment to be chief.

Herbert said the city will advertise the position nationally, similar to the procedure that is used by City Council in filling top management jobs.

But he indicated that the city also will consider applicants from within the Fire Department in filling the job that now pays more than $40,000.

"We owe it to this community to look both internally and externally to find the best person for this job," he said.

Rawleigh Quarles
Accepts new assignment

Herbert said Kerley had submitted his resignation last April — to be effective Oct. 5. The city manager accepted the resignation then, but he agreed to keep it secret until Kerley was ready to make it public.

Kerley will remain with the city until October to serve as an assistant to George Snead, director of administration and public safety.

Quarles, who had been fire marshal and deputy chief for technical services, was appointed deputy chief for training and safety two weeks ago.

Kerley made the reassignment as part of a reshuffling of the top management in the department. Kerley said he reassigned Quarles because he needed him to oversee training.

Quarles was unhappy with the move and reportedly has considered contesting it.

But Herbert said he has met with Quarles and the deputy chief has withdrawn his complaint about the reassignment.

Asked why Kerley had been allowed to reassign the deputy chiefs even after he had resigned, Herbert said Kerley was still chief with the right to make the changes.

Quarles said he has accepted the reassignment as deputy chief for training and safety.

Please see **Search**, Page **B2**

Search

From Page B1

Quarles didn't want to comment further or say whether Kerley's resignation had influenced his position on his reassignment. Quarles also wouldn't say whether he will seek the chief's job.

When the controversy arose earlier over the reassignment, Herbert said he considered Quarles' new job to be a "positive" move that could better prepare him for possible future promotions.

Quarles has done a good job as fire marshal and deputy chief for technical services, Herbert said.

Without commenting directly on Quarles, Herbert said then that the city's management approach is to give "supervisory people as wide experience as possible so they work in a number of areas so they can position themselves to compete successfully in the future for higher management jobs."

Herbert denied that Kerley's resignation was linked to unrest and controversy in the Fire Department in the past year.

Councilmen Robert Garland and James Harvey said they didn't object to Herbert's decision to allow Kerley to remain with the city until October.

Snead said Kerley will be doing special assignments for him, including working on the implementation of the Emergency 911 phone system that will go line in October.

When Kerley submitted his resignation last April, Herbert said, he agreed to let him stay in the job for six months because he thought it was a fair arrangement.

Herbert said he also offered then to help Kerley find a new job.

He didn't tell City Council about Kerley's resignation until shortly before it was announced Friday.

Garland said he couldn't blame Herbert for keeping the resignation secret until now or agreeing to let him stay on six months.

"I believe what Mr. Herbert was trying to do was to do as little harm as possible to Mr. Kerley's future job possibilities," Garland said.

"He was trying to give him six months to find a job."

City fire chief job still unfilled

By JOEL TURNER
MUNICIPAL WRITER

The Roanoke fire chief's job has not been offered to anyone, according to a city official, although several applicants have reportedly been interviewed for the position.

George Snead, director of administration and public safety, said Thursday that no one has been offered the position despite speculation that city officials may bring in an outsider.

Snead refused to confirm or deny that city officials have interviewed at least one applicant from outside the Roanoke Valley.

Don Shelton, a retired fire captain, said he has learned that Snead and other officials have made at least one trip to another state to interview an applicant for the job.

Several firefighters who did not want to be identified said they also had heard that city officials are considering applicants from outside the Fire Department.

Shelton said he doesn't understand why city officials would interview out-of-town applicants because there are qualified applicants within the department.

Rawleigh Quarles, deputy fire chief for training, should get the job, Shelton said.

"If anyone ever deserved the chief's job, it is Quarles. They don't need to be going outside to hire a chief."

Quarles and Billy Akers, deputy chief for administration, have served as acting chief since Harry McKinney retired for health reasons last December after serving as chief less than two years.

Akers served as acting chief for the first three months after McKinney's departure. Quarles has been acting chief the past three months.

Akers and Quarles are thought to be contenders for the job. The plan for each to serve as acting chief for three months was discussed with them when McKinney retired.

"We have two senior deputy chiefs and we thought this arrangement would give both a chance to have experience as acting chief," Snead said earlier.

Quarles wouldn't comment today.

The city received 169 applications for the chief's job. It advertised the position in national publications as well as locally.

When McKinney retired, Snead said that the city would have open competition for the job and wouldn't restrict it to applicants from within the Fire Department.

When Jerry Kerley was hired in 1983, there was controversy because he didn't come from within the ranks. Kerley had been fire chief in Albemarle, N.C., before coming to Roanoke.

The Roanoke Fire Fighters Association, the firefighters' union, and several City Council members said then that they thought that the new chief should have come from within the ranks.

Kerley resigned under pressure in 1987 during a controversy about his personal life.

"It looks like city officials would have learned a lesson in going outside to hire a chief," Shelton said.

It is the third time in the past six years that the city has conducted a search for a new fire chief.

Roanoke City Manager Robert Herbert (left) announces Rawleigh Quarles' appointment as fire chief Thursday

JACK GAKING/Staff

Roanoke names black fire chief

By JOEL TURNER
MUNICIPAL WRITER

Rawleigh Quarles reached the top of the Roanoke Fire Department on Thursday, but it wasn't an easy climb.

Quarles, the city's first black firefighter, was named fire chief, more than two decades after he started as a 21-year-old firefighter.

His climb through the department's ranks has been sometimes difficult and controversial.

As a young firefighter, Quarles fought racial discrimination, both inside and outside the Fire Department.

He filed a discrimination complaint against the city in the 1970s that won him a promotion to fire marshal and $14,000 in back pay.

In an interview several years ago, Quarles recalled one experience as a black firefighter in the 1960s, when segregation was still the rule in some of Roanoke's restaurants.

After a downtown blaze had been brought under control on a cold day in 1964, a fire commander suggested that Quarles and several other firemen visit a nearby business for coffee.

Inside the restaurant, the white firefighters received their coffee in porcelain mugs. Quarles got his in a Styrofoam cup.

But Quarles, 47, said Thursday that "there has been a tremendous improvement" in racial relations both within and outside the department since he began as a firefighter in 1963.

He said he hopes that color wasn't a factor in his selection from among 169 applicants for the job.

City Manager Robert Herbert said that he chose Quarles because he has the management skills and experience needed for the job.

The department has 243 employees and an $8.5 million budget.

"This is one of the largest departments in the city and requires good management skills. Rawleigh Quarles meets that criteria," Herbert said.

"The fire chief's job is one of the toughest half-dozen jobs in the city," Herbert said. "We have a good department with an excellent senior management team, but I need a good strong manager for that department."

The city now has more than 20 black firefighters. Quarles said he is confident that Herbert and the city administration fully support equal employment for blacks.

Quarles' promotion was effective Thursday and his starting salary will be $47,000.

He began the new job by visiting fire stations and talking with firefighters on duty. Quarles said he hoped to visit all of the city's 13 stations by the end of the day.

CHAPTER 11

All Glory, Honor, Thanks, and Praise Belongs to God for Allowing Me to Climb the Ladder of Success and Reach My Journey to the Top

After much prayer and seeking to know the will of God, He revealed to me His divine purpose and will for my life. It was to proclaim the gospel of Jesus Christ and preach the Word of God. Shortly after accepting or acknowledging my call to the preaching ministry, I had a meeting with the city manager and thanked him for his trust and confidence he had placed in me in appointing me fire chief. I also informed him that he had to name another fire chief because God had a higher calling for me than that of fire chief.

I opted for an early retirement, and on February 25, 1995, I retired as Fire Chief for the City of Roanoke Fire Department and became full time pastor for the Staunton Avenue Church of God in Roanoke, Virginia. As of the writing of this book, I am still currently serving in this capacity.

Chapter 11 closes out thirty-one years and three months of my career as a public servant, focusing on the physical, human, and natural needs of man. Chapter 12 begins with me still serving as a servant of mankind, in which I was not only focusing on the physical, human, and natural needs of man, but in addition, also the spiritual needs of man as well. The wholistic man, both physical and spiritual.

This chapter ends the secular phase of my career as I climbed the ladder of success and journeyed to the top, and the beginning of my spiritual journey for Jesus Christ and my Heavenly Father, to proclaim the infallible, God-breathed, and Eternal Word of God.

Roanoke names Quarles fire chief

By JOEL TURNER
MUNICIPAL WRITER

Rawleigh W. Quarles, Roanoke's first black firefighter, was named city fire chief today, ending a climb through the Fire Department's ranks that began more than two decades ago.

Quarles was selected from a pool of 169 applicants that included finalists from within and outside the city Fire Department.

City Manager Robert Herbert said that he chose Quarles because he has the management skills and experience that he was seeking in a chief.

"In looking for a new fire chief, I wanted an individual who could continue to work to strengthen our primary mission of saving lives and property," Herbert said at a news conference.

"This is one of the largest departments in the city and requires good management skills. Rawleigh Quarles meets that criteria."

Herbert said that Quarles is the kind of leader he was seeking to oversee the operations of the Fire Department, which has 243 employees and an $8.5 million budget.

Quarles' promotion to chief is effective today and his starting salary will be $47,000.

Quarles, 47, has shared the job of acting chief since the retirement of former chief Harry McKinney last December. From December until March 15, Billy Akers, deputy chief for administration and technical services, was acting chief. Quarles has been acting chief since then.

Akers was one of the three finalists who were interviewed for the chief's job. The third unidentified finalist came from outside the city, according to George Snead, director of administration and public safety.

Quarles joined the city in 1963 as a firefighter and was promoted to lieutenant and fire inspector in 1973. In 1979, he became a captain and fire marshal in 1979. He was named deputy chief for technical services and chief fire marshal in 1985. Two years later, he became deputy chief for training and safety.

As deputy chief for training, Quarles had responsibility for overall training in the department, a key job where he refined the manage-

Rawleigh W. Quarles
Selected from 169 applicants

PLEASE SEE **QUARLES**/A8

7-13-89

Quarles new city fire chief

By JOEL TURNER
MUNICIPAL WRITER

Rawleigh Quarles reached the top of the Roanoke Fire Department on Thursday, but it wasn't an easy climb.

Quarles, the city's first black firefighter, was named fire chief, more than two decades after he started as a 21-year-old firefighter.

His climb through the department's ranks has been sometimes difficult and controversial.

As a young firefighter, Quarles fought racial discrimination, both inside and outside the Fire Department.

He filed a discrimination complaint against the city in the 1970s that won him a promotion to fire marshal and $14,000 in back pay.

In an interview several years ago, Quarles recalled one experience as a black firefighter in the 1960s, when segregation was still the rule in some of Roanoke's restaurants.

After a downtown blaze had been brought under control on a cold day in 1964, a fire commander suggested that Quarles and several other firemen visit a nearby business for coffee.

Inside the restaurant, the white firefighters received their coffee in porcelain mugs. Quarles got his in a Styrofoam cup.

But Quarles, 47, said Thursday that "there has been a tremendous improvement" in racial relations both within and outside the department since he began as a firefighter in 1963.

He said he hopes that color wasn't a factor in his selection from among 169 applicants for the job.

He said he hopes he was selected for his skills and experience, not because of his race or past clashes with city officials.

City Manager Robert Herbert said that he chose Quarles because he has the management skills and experience needed for the job.

The department has 243 employees and an $8.5 million budget.

PLEASE SEE **QUARLES**/A10

7-16-90

Fire chief finds his first year a good one

By JOEL TURNER
MUNICIPAL WRITER

After a year as Roanoke's fire chief, Rawleigh Quarles says he's beginning to feel almost comfortable.

He's become familiar with the responsibilities and requirements of the job.

He's learned what it's like to supervise one of the largest municipal departments, with a $9.3 million budget and 245 employees.

He thinks a majority of the city's firefighters has accepted him as chief.

He said his first year has been challenging and rewarding. It's been what he expected, and he has no regrets about accepting the position.

But he quickly adds, "Maybe I shouldn't say I'm getting comfortable because it could indicate [I'm] taking too much for granted."

Quarles, the city's first black chief, has learned never to take anything for granted. He has worked too hard and struggled too much in his 27 years in the Fire Department to assume anything.

His climb through the ranks was sometimes difficult and controversial. As a young firefighter, he fought discrimination, both inside and outside the department.

Quarles, 48, started as a 21-year-old firefighter in 1963 when segregation was still the rule in some of Roanoke's restaurants.

After a downtown fire had been brought under control on a cold winter

PLEASE SEE **CHIEF**/A8

Rawleigh Quarles
Quick response his top priority

Chief

FROM PAGE A3

day in 1964, a fire commander suggested that Quarles and several other firefighters visit a nearby business for coffee.

Inside the restaurant, the white firefighters received their coffee in porcelain mugs. Quarles got his in a plastic foam cup.

In the 1970s, Quarles filed a racial discrimination complaint against the city that won him a promotion to fire marshal and $14,000 in back pay.

But the days of segregation and controversy are behind him. The city now has more than 20 black firefighters. And Quarles is confident that City Manager Robert Herbert and top city administrators fully support equal employment opportunities for blacks.

It's been a busy year. He has:

■ Reviewed the city's firefighting equipment needs. A committee he appointed recommended that the city spend more than $2 million on new fire trucks and other emergency vehicles. City officials are reviewing the list.

■ Planned for a new fire station in the rapidly growing U.S. 460 corridor, which is expected to be finished by the fall of 1991.

■ Upgraded management training for the department's top command staff.

■ Instituted standardized training for all firefighters and started a physical fitness program.

■ Developed a so-called first responder program for using firefighters to answer emergency rescue calls in some neighborhoods.

■ Worked out a mutual aid agreement with Roanoke County for responding to fire calls at retirement homes near the city-county line.

And at the same time, he's concentrated on his main responsibility: making sure the city's firefighters responded quickly to more than 3,000 fire and emergency calls.

Quarles was chosen from among 170 applicants for the job. Herbert said he selected him because he had the management skills and experience for the job.

"The fire chief's job is one of the toughest half-dozen jobs in the city," Herbert said. "We have a good department with an excellent senior management team, but I need a good strong manager for that department."

Top city officials are pleased with Quarles' performance as chief, according to George Snead, city director of administration and public safety. Quarles has "a clear vision of where he, the city manager and I want the department to go," said Snead, the chief's immediate supervisor.

"He's focusing on developing a strong management team, better training and professional development of the staff — and how the department can provide more services as we head into the 1990s and the 21st century," Snead said.

"He is setting a high standard for himself and the department. He's very demanding of himself and he's demanding of others, but he has matured as a departmental leader in the past year."

The city's firehouses, which buzzed with controversy in the 1980s, have been generally quiet since Quarles became chief. The department was in turmoil for several years preceding the forced resignation of Jerry Kerley as chief in 1987 because of complaints about his personal life and charges of favoritism in promotions.

Harry McKinney, who succeeded Kerley, retired, partly for health reasons, less than two years after becoming chief.

Quarles thinks morale among the firefighters has improved in the past 12 months. "I certainly see an improvement in attitudes, professionalism and the conduct of our personnel. They are taking pride in their careers, responsibilities and the organization," he said.

There is lingering disappointment among some firefighters because Billy Akers, deputy chief for administration and technical services, did not get the top job, according to several firefighters who did not want to be identified.

Some firefighters think Akers should have been named chief because he had more on-line experience as a firefighter and command officer, but they have accepted the decision.

"Morale is not great, but it's not bad, either," said one firefighter.

Akers and Quarles were the two finalists for the job. Each served as acting chief for three months before Herbert chose Quarles. Akers would not comment when Quarles was named chief, and he would not comment for this story.

Although there has been no controversy over promotions since Quarles became chief, one unexpected change has occurred in the department's top command staff.

Bev Mitchell, who was promoted from a district chief to deputy chief for operations soon after Quarles became chief, asked to be reassigned to his old job a month later. Mitchell would not comment on the reasons for his decision.

Quarles said he hopes to win the confidence and respect of the department's 245 employees by what he does and how he does it. To him, acceptance and respect are something to be earned, not given simply because of his position.

"I have to prove my competence, my ability, my leadership and job knowledge — and that I am honest and fair. If you prove those things, acceptance is not so hard to get," he said.

Quarles said he has received excellent cooperation from the city's top management officials and other municipal departments.

There is no evidence that his past clashes with city officials on the racial discrimination charge and the need to fill vacant fire inspector jobs have had hurt his relations with other officials since he became chief. These incidents occurred before Herbert became city manager.

As chief, Quarles said he stresses teamwork among the command staff and firefighters.

"I don't care if it is a first-year firefighter. He has ideas, he has recommendations, and we need to listen to him," Quarles said. "We need to hear him, and he needs to feel a part of this organization."

7-15-89

NEW FIRE CHIEF

Quarles reaches top on merit

TWO YEARS ago, in a reshuffling of duties among deputy fire chiefs, Rawleigh Quarles appeared to be getting a raw deal. He had done a good job as fire marshal and deputy chief for technical services, where he had acquired supervisory experience. When the deputy chief for operations retired, Quarles wanted to move into that position.

Instead, Quarles was given the assignment of deputy chief for training and safety, which involved less supervisory responsibility than his old job. Quarles was unhappy. But City Manager Robert Herbert said Quarles' new assignment would broaden his background and leave him better qualified for future promotion.

If that was a semi-promise, the city manager came through with a full delivery. On Thursday, after considering a list of 169 applicants from inside the department and outside, Herbert named Quarles to the $47,000-a-year job of city fire chief. By all accounts, the 47-year-old veteran is well-qualified for the position.

It should be only a footnote that Quarles is the city's first black fire chief, but that distinction deserves more than passing comment. Quarles was also the city's first black firefighter. During the '70s, he fought and won a racial discrimination fight with the city. As a result, he was promoted to fire marshal and awarded $14,000 in back pay.

He followed up his success in the suit with success as an administrator. Herbert says he chose Quarles because the new chief has the management skills and experience needed to manage a department of 243 employees and a budget of $8.5 million.

Quarles says he hopes race wasn't a factor in his elevation to the top job. He no longer believes the city to be following discriminatory hiring policies. Among his subordinates are 20 black firefighters. There's no reason to believe Quarles would not have won the job on merit had he been of another race.

Roanoke can be proud of the example it sets in race relations. When a Southern city that is 77 percent white consistently elects a black mayor, hires topflight black administrators and installs a black person as fire chief, it testifies to a healthy racial attitude.

Friday, July 14, 1989

Quarles

FROM PAGE A1

"This is one of the largest departments in the city and requires good management skills. Rawleigh Quarles meets that criteria," Herbert said.

"The fire chief's job is one of the toughest half-dozen jobs in the city," Herbert said. "We have a good department with an excellent senior management team, but I need a good strong manager for that department."

The city now has more than 20 black firemen. Quarles said he is confident that Herbert and the city administration fully support equal employment for blacks.

Quarles' promotion was effective Thursday and his starting salary will be $47,000.

He began the new job by visiting fire stations and talking with firefighters on duty. Quarles said he hoped to visit all of the city's 13 stations by the end of the day.

"My desire is to effectively and efficiently lead the city's Fire Department. I hope to help enhance the professionalism, pride, enthusiasm and leadership qualities of the members of the organization as we work together to provide the highest level of fire protection for citizens and property," Quarles said.

Despite turmoil in the department in recent years with the resignation of Jerry Kerley as chief in 1987 and the retirement of his successor, Harry McKinney, last December, Quarles said that morale among the firemen in good.

"I am not concerned about that. We have a staff that is totally committed to working together and providing the best fire protection possible," Quarles said.

Capt. Richard Sarver, a former president of the Roanoke Firefighters Association, said most firemen seemed happy that the new chief has come from within the department.

Quarles has shared the job of acting chief since the retirement of McKinney. From December until March 15, Billy Akers, deputy chief for administration and technical services, was acting chief. Quarles has been acting chief since then.

Akers was one of the three finalists interviewed. The third, unidentified, finalist came from outside the city, according to George Snead, director of administration and public safety.

Quarles was promoted to lieutenant and fire inspector in 1973. In 1977, he became a captain and fire marshal. He was named deputy chief for technical services and chief fire marshal in 1985. Two years later, he became deputy chief for training and safety.

Almost 10 years after joining the Fire Department, Quarles complained that he didn't get the fire marshal's job because he was black. He maintained that he was more qualified than the white man who got it and filed a complaint with the federal Equal Employment Opportunity Commission.

The EEOC ruled that the city had discriminated against Quarles and other black firefighters. The result was that Quarles was promoted to fire marshal in 1977 and given $14,000 in back pay. Roanoke's other black firefighters received a cash settlement from the city after the ruling.

But Quarles said that he never considered himself to be an agitator despite his clash with city officials.

"I never thought I'd be playing that sort of role, but when I saw my constitutional rights were being violated.... I was going to pursue this matter to its conclusion," Quarles said, in an interview several years ago.

Quarles also battled with city administrators again in 1982 when he sued the city and asked that a grievance panel hear his complaint that two vacant fire inspector jobs be filled. Administrators decided to fill the open slots while the grievance was pending.

Quarles is a graduate of the former Lucy Addison High School and has taken courses in fire science a Virginia Western Community College and the National Fire Academy in Emmitsburg, Md. He has been certified by the state as a fire inspector III and fire/arson investigator III, the highest attainable level. In addition, he is certified as an adjunct fire instructor.

Quarles is a member of the Building Officials and Code Administrators International, the International Association of Arson Investigators and the National Association for the Advancement of Colored People. He is married to the former Barbara Ann Girst; the couple has one daughter, Nicole, 14, and two sons, Rawleigh Jr., 24, and Derrick 19.

Sr. Fire Officer Completes Executive Program

EMMITSBURG, MD--The National Fire Academy (NFA) has announced that Chief Rawleigh W. Quarles, Sr. successfully completed the Executive Fire Officer Program (EFOP).

"The intensive EFOP is designed to provide senior fire officers with a broad perspective on various facets of fire administration," according to NFA Acting Superintendent James F. Coyle. "This program provides fire service officers with the expertise they need to succeed in today's challenging environment."

Each of the courses required a written Applied Research Project (ARP) to demonstrate application of course theory and concepts to real life situations within the student's own organization. Each of these projects was evaluated through a formal process, and progression through the program was contingent on achieving each of these milestones.

Six months after the completion of each of the four courses, the EFOP participants were required to complete an ARP in their own organization. The required executive-level courses are:

"Executive Development," the entry level course, emphasizes team developmetn and consensus decisionmaking to enhance organizational effectiveness.

The next course in the sequence, "Executive Analysis for Fire Service Operations in Emergency Management' provides fire executives with a series of actual large-scale incidents.

RAWLEIGH QUARLES

(Continued on Page 6)

Senior Fire Officer

(Continued from Page 1)

This "lessons learned" approach is presented in the context of using an effective command management system to mitigate the incident.

"Strategic Analysis of Community Risk Reduction," is the third course in the series. It focuses on the attitudes and values of the senior fire executive towards fire prevention, public education, and code enforcement activities.

The final course, "Executive Leadership," examines all aspects of executive-level leadership and ties together the educational experiences of the three previous years.

NFA offers a wide array of programs and courses for fire service and allied professions. Courses are delivered on campus as well as throughout the Nation in coordination with State and local fire training officials and local colleges and universities.

Chief Quarles is the first City of Roanoke Fire Department member to attend the academie's Executive fire Officers Course, and is one of only 29 Fire Department Officers in the Commonwealth to this date to graduate as an Executive Fire Officer.

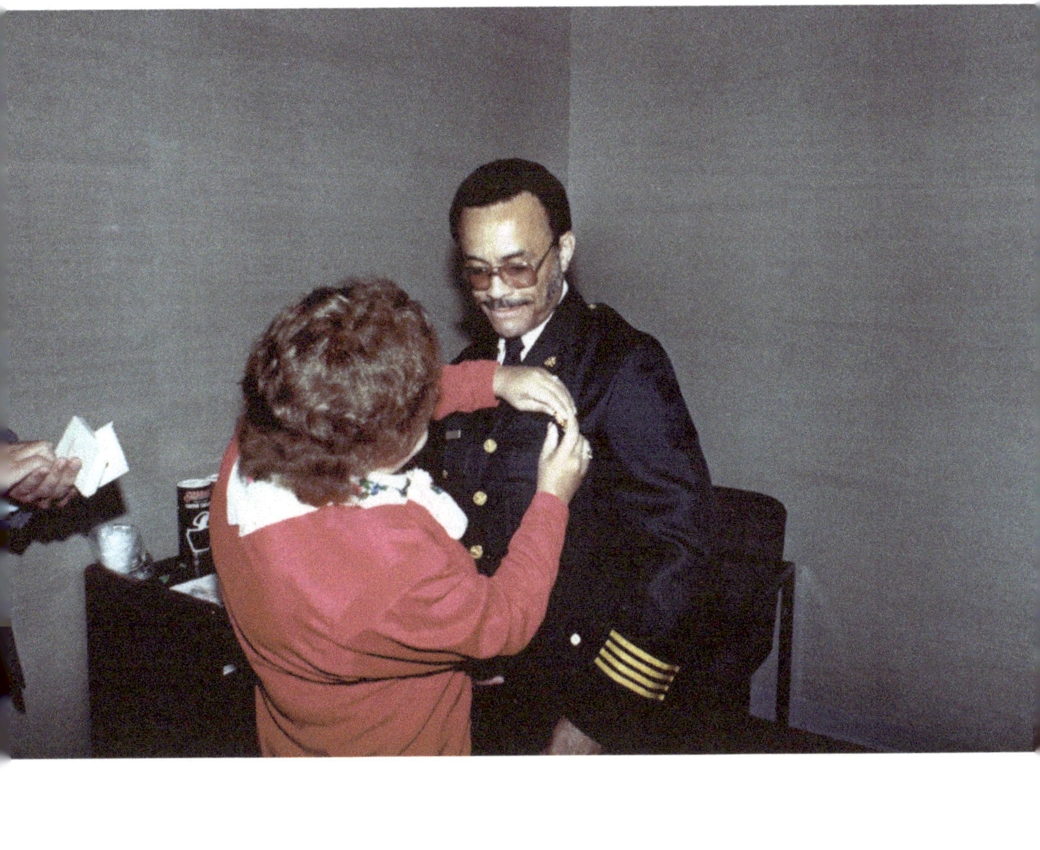

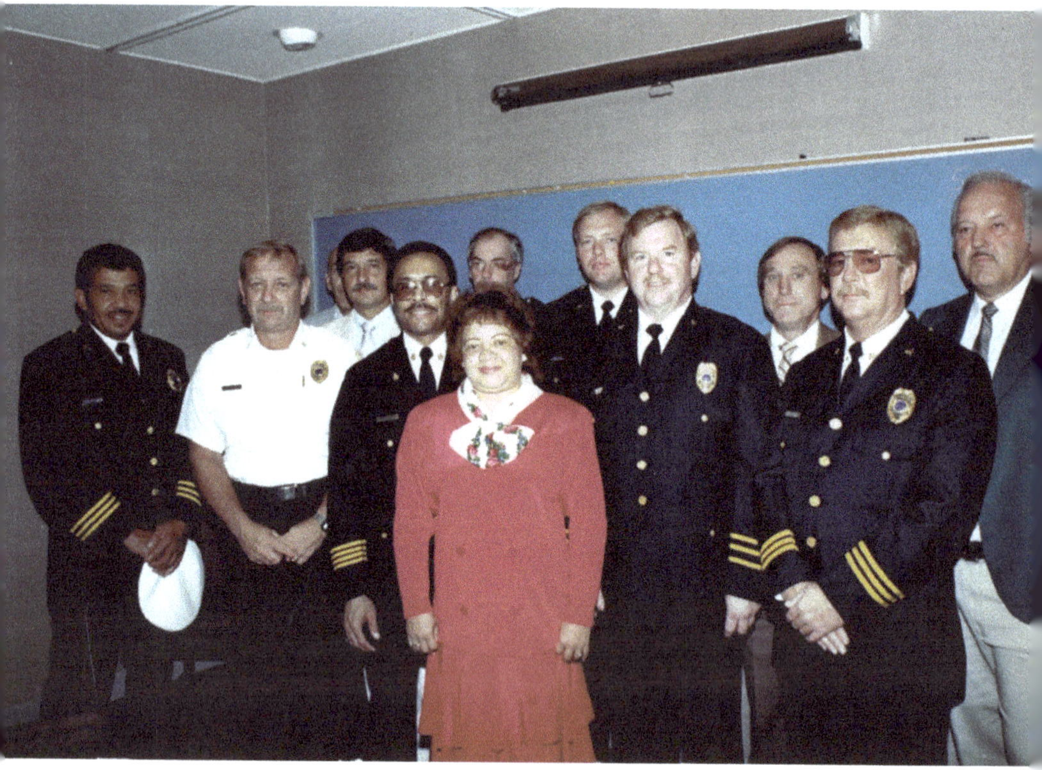

CITY of
DEPARTMENT
CHIEF
OPERATI
ADMINISTRATION
PREVENT
TRAINING & SAFETY
NING

Federal Emergency Management Agency
United States Fire Administration
National Fire Academy
Emmitsburg, Maryland 21727

Dear Executive Fire Officer Program Graduate:

Congratulations! You have successfully completed all of the curriculum and research requirements of the National Fire Academy's (NFA) "Executive Fire Officer Program" (EFOP).

The enclosed certificate is testimony of your professional commitment to career development, organizational improvement, and the fire service at large. Executive fire officers have a tremendous responsibility to lead and guide both organizations and committees through changing times. Your contributions to self-development and academic research will be long lasting. I know that you will display this certificate proudly. It is our desire that you continue to engage in lifelong learning that will benefit your community and your personal development.

Again, on behalf of the faculty and staff, I extend my warmest congratulations and thank you for your continuing support of the NFA and its programs.

Sincerely,

James F. Coyle
Acting Superintendent

Enclosure

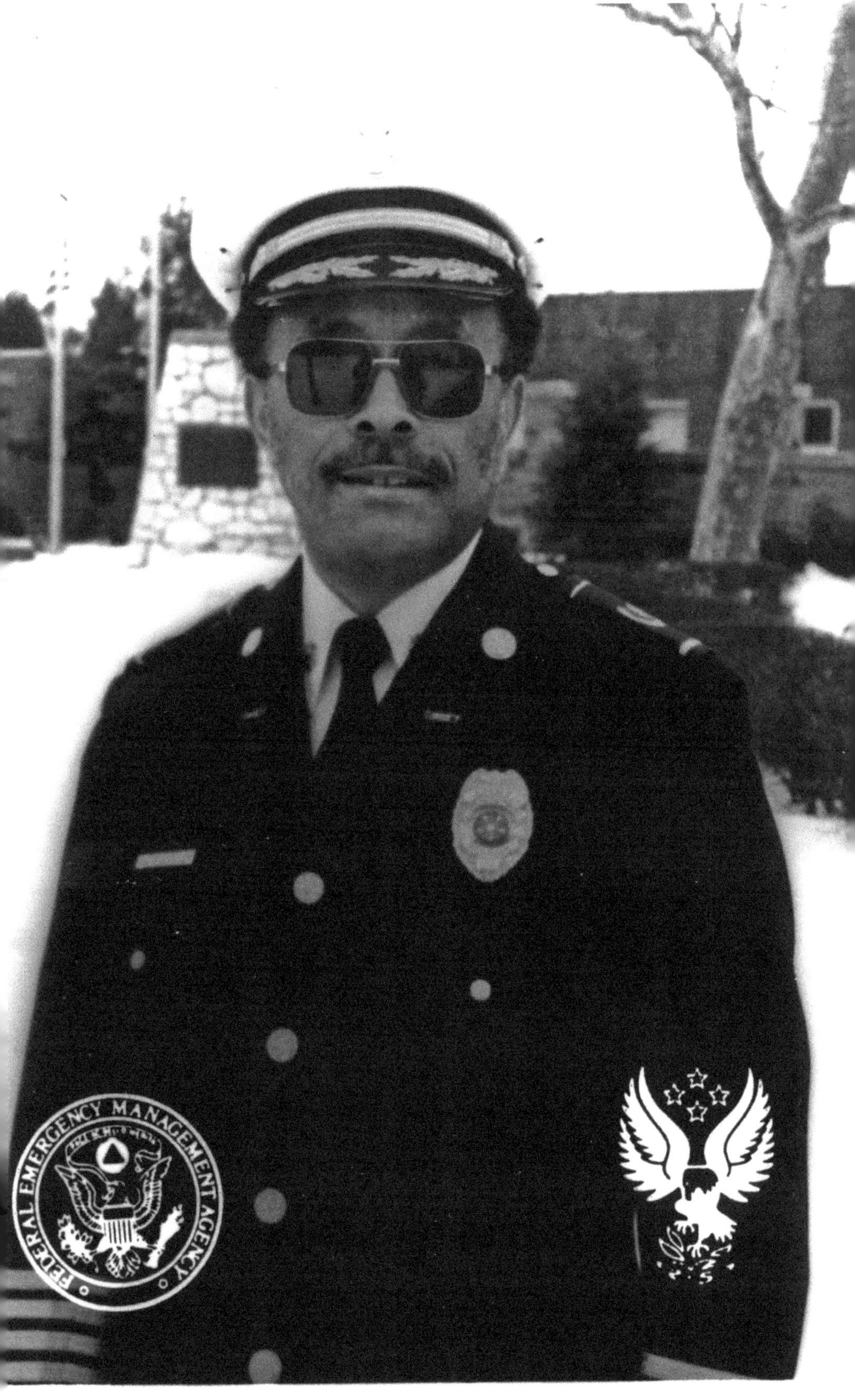
FEDERAL EMERGENCY MANAGEMENT AGENCY

Fire chief glad he can get back to work

A YEAR AFTER *some of his own men made allegations that led to a state police probe which eventually exonerated him, Roanoke's fire chief wants to talk about his job, not himself.*

By JOEL TURNER
STAFF WRITER

Roanoke Fire Chief Rawleigh Quarles is busy, but he's not complaining.

He's grappling with budget cuts while he seeks to expand the Fire Department's services.

He's searching for ways to trim the department's budget for the fiscal year that begins July 1. Because of tight finances, each city department must prepare alternative spending plans showing the impact of cuts of various amounts.

Quarles also is trying to recruit women and more black firefighters for the 244-member department. The department has no female firefighters, and only about 10 percent are black.

He also is overseeing a study of the location of the city's 14 fire stations and whether some need to be relocated or more need to be built.

As if that's not enough to keep him busy, he is expanding the department's "first-responder" program so more firefighters can answer emergency medical calls.

At four fire stations on the outskirts of the city, firefighters with emergency-medical training answer first-aid calls and stay until paramedics can take over. The program will be expanded to a fifth station next year.

Despite the hectic schedule, Quarles said he is doing what he enjoys. He would rather be working than trying to defend his own integrity.

A year ago, Quarles was spending much of his time answering allegations that he had misused state funds, rigged bids on fire trucks and accepted improper gratuities from a fire-engine company.

State police spent three months investigating him, but no charges were placed. Roanoke Commonwealth's Attorney Donald Caldwell said Quarles had shown poor judgment, but that there was no evidence to support criminal charges.

Quarles, who has been chief nearly

PLEASE SEE QUARLES/C3

Chief Raleigh Quarles is overseeing a study of Roanoke's 14 fire stations.

LONNIE TIMMONS III/Staff

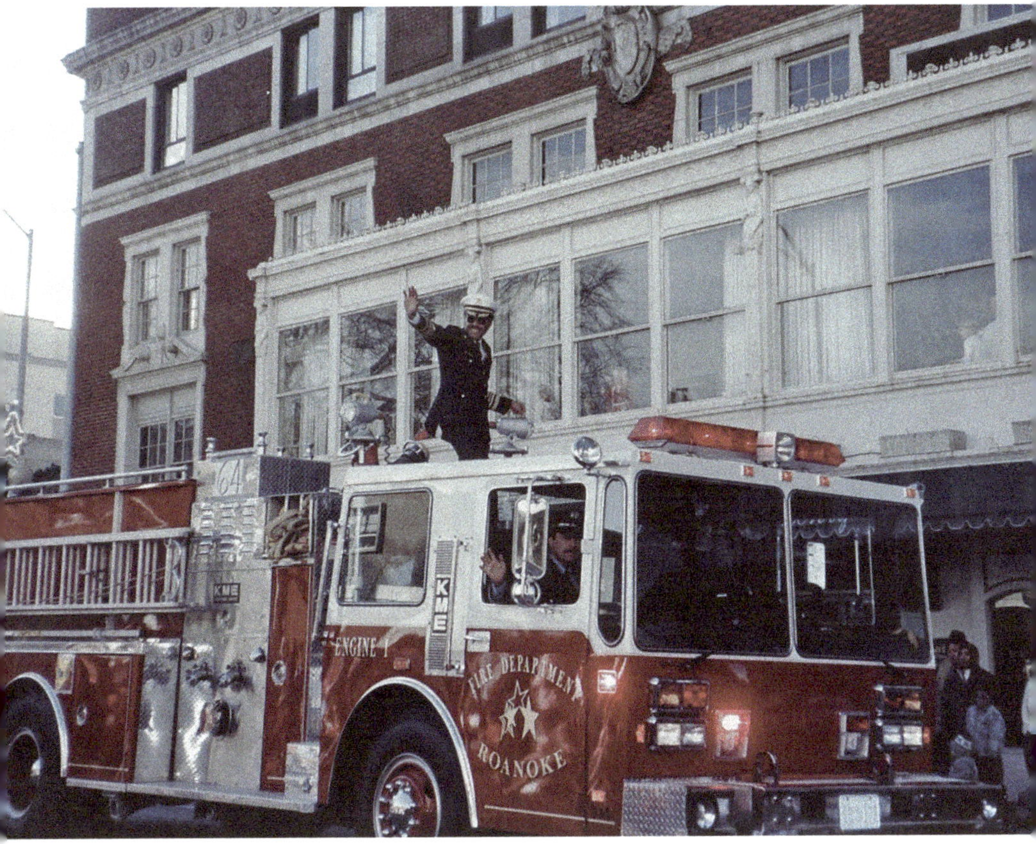
64
KME
KME
ENGINE 1
FIRE DEPARTMENT
ROANOKE

CHAPTER **12**

Confirmation or Validation of God's Divine Call to Proclaim the Word of God or to the Preaching Ministry

About two years prior to graduation from the National Fire Academy and before I announced my retirement, I was enrolled in the National Fire Academy's Executive Fire Officer's Program of Emmetsburg, Maryland. The program required four years attendance – two weeks per year to graduate. I would leave the academy after the first week each year of attendance and return home for the weekend and speak at my church as an ordained Deacon. It was during my last year of attendance that I felt a strong leading of the Lord in or on my life. During the last two weeks of classes before graduation, I found myself in sincere prayer, dedication, consecration, devotion, and commitment regarding God's will for my life.

It was during the last week before graduation that I was convinced that it was God's will for me to accept His divine call to the preaching ministry. Now the question was how my wife was going to receive this news. I will never forget that Sundays worship experience. By Sundays 11:00 am service, I had not mentioned a word about it to my wife.

When it was time to speak, I walked into the pulpit, took my place behind the podium/dais, opened my Bible, and began speaking. Notice, I did not say "preaching," for at this time I had not acknowledged God's call to the preaching ministry to the congregation. As I continued to speak, I suddenly experienced a divine and anointed presence and power of God that had come upon me. It filled the sanctuary, and it was at that moment that I knew that my "speaking" had transitioned to that of "preaching." Not only did I feel God's anointing, but I could also sense His divine presence and power on those in attendance.

After benediction, as I calmly but humbly exited the sanctuary, and my wife and I walked to our vehicle, she looked at me and said, "you had them under a spell today, didn't you?" I said to her, what do you mean (as if I did not know what she meant). She responded to me with the second question, "God hasn't called you to the ministry, has He?!" I said yes and she said, "take me home." God had intervened and resolved what I thought would be a difficult task of breaking the news to her, as God would have it so to speak, she broke the news to me. What a confirmation and validation of Gods' call in my life.

Sometimes later, after I had been serving an extended trial period for the church for several months (at my request), both I and my wife were concerned as to whether it was Gods' will for me to pastor the church. The church's desire was that I become pastor and I stated that God had called me to the ministry, but that He had not called me to pastor the church. After serving for approximately a year on a trial basis, another validation and confirmation took place. I was still serving as Fire Chief. Both of us were still praying regarding Gods' will, and God validated as well as confirmed to me that it was His will for me to pastor the church. I did not share the revelation with my wife immediately, hoping that God would intervene and reveal His will to her also. God worked in mysterious ways then, and He still works in mysterious ways; His wonders to perform. Another confirmation and validation of Gods' will in both our lives!

One morning as I was shaving, my wife was sitting on the edge of the bed, and she said to me, Rawleigh, I think it's God's will for you to pastor the church." That was my very thought that I had not shared with her at the time. See how God had confirmed His will not only to me, but to my wife as well. Another confirmation or validation of God's divine call in my life, as well as to my wife, to accept serving as a pastor's wife. There was a congregational vote as to me being approved as pastor elect, and guess what, the vote was unanimous for me to become pastor. Do you see God's confirmation and validation?

God was not finished with me yet! I faced yet another test of my faith in God. If I would take early retirement, to pastor the church full time, would I be able to adjust to the financial loss? My salary as Fire Chief topped out at $54,000.00 annually. The church salary was $12,000.00 annually. In addition, I would be penalized if I took early retirement and would not receive full benefit unless I had achieved thirty-five years of service. At the time, I had only 31+ years service.

God was still working on me, refining me, with yet another test of my faith. I was at home recovering from cancer surgery with 2 weeks of sick leave left. The cancer was discovered one year after I had accepted God's call to the ministry. How's that for timing?! I must admit that this was a frightening realization. After much prayer and thought, I decided to trust God and in faith, put Him first in my life. I was assured that He would take care of my needs according to His riches in glory. Two weeks after making that commitment to God, He intervened. He miraculously indicated that He had it all under control, and that He would provide for my financial need, as well as all other needs. We must prove to God that we love Him more than anything else in our life, and always put Him first. He will have first place or no place. Some of you know the Biblical story of Abraham and Isaac (Genesis Chapter 22). Only after Abraham proved to God that his love for God was greater than his love for his son Isaac, did God intervene, and provided another sacrifice or a ram in the bush.

Confirmation or Validation of God's Divine Call

As I mentioned, I had two weeks remaining on sick leave when my telephone rang, during the time I was away from home, so my wife answered the telephone, and it was one of my Deputy Chiefs'. He told my wife to tell the chief that "what he had been hoping for, in taking early retirement has come to pass, and that he can retire without being penalized on his pension." When I returned home, my wife related the good news to me. The city had adopted a new pension plan that afforded early retirement for those who wanted to opt out for early retirement. This was a one-time offer to allow those employees with twenty-five years of service or more to retire without penalty. At that time, I had 31+ years of service. To have remained as an employee, under the old plan for four or more years (someone calculated it would have taken me thirteen more years of service), in order for me to have received the pension that the new plan offered. If I had chosen to take the new plan and not retire, my pension benefits would not have increased. Of course, I opted for the new plan and chose early retirement. To this day, God has supplied all my needs according to His riches in glory! God works in mysterious ways. Another confirmation or validation of Gods' call. If God leads you to it, He will lead you through it.

Roanoke *Tribune* City Fire Chief Announces Retirement

Roanoke City Fire Chief Rawleigh W. Quarles, Sr., today announced that he will retire effective March 1, 1995. Quarles, who is a licensed and ordained minister, will focus his efforts on the ministry. He currently serves as the pastor of the Staunton Avenue Church of God.

Quarles has 31 years of service with the Roanoke City Fire Department. He started as a firefighter in 1963, was promoted to lieutenant and became a fire inspector in 1972, followed by a promotion to deputy chief/fire marshal in 1977. He became deputy chief of Training in 1987 and was named Roanoke City Fire Chief in 1989.

"Rawleigh Quarles has a significant history of contributions to the city of Roanoke and its citizens," said City Manager Bob Herbert. "We wish him the very best as he pursues his other calling."

Under Quarles direction as fire chief the Fire Department made numerous positive strides including:

• Initiating an equipment replacement program which resulted in the purchase of over $2.25 million worth of vehicles and equipment for the Fire Department. This reduced the average age of department vehicles from 25 years to 15 years.

• Constructed Fire Station #14 in the 460 East Corridor to address service needs in that area.

• Introduced the First Responder Program, whereby firefighters at specific stations provide first response to calls for medical assistance until the ambulance arrives. It is now in effect at six stations and has greatly improved response time and service to customers.

• Initiated Officer Leadership Training, ongoing standardized Fire Tower Evolution Training and a customer service program within the Fire Department.

• Began a physical fitness program for all firefighters and hired a new airport training/health fitness officer.

• To assist in the recruitment of minorities and women in the firefighting profession, introduced a Firefighter Cadet Program whereby high school students get class credit and certification in firefighting skills.

"For over a year, I have devoted my off-work hours to my ministry," said Quarles who became an interim pastor in June 1993, and then was ordained and installed as a full-time pastor in May 1994. "My retirement from the city will allow more time to tend to the needs of my congregation. In many ways, I'm just changing my focus from one flock to another."

Quarles said he decided to announce his retirement now in order to give the city as much advance notice as possible to begin the search for his successor and to help ensure a smooth transition. He added that a new retirement option recently approved by City Council was also an incentive. Under the option, all employees in the city's "old" retirement system will have the option to move into the new retirement system, which in some cases can provide greater benefits.

RAWLEIGH QUARLES

CHAPTER **13**

Fire Chief Announces Retirement

I have in the last twelve chapters chronologically brought you to chapter 13 and now the final chapter, chapter 14, which closes or ends this autobiography. Chapter 13 ends my secular career and chapter 14 begins my spiritual journey as a minister of the gospel. Even after my ministry comes to an end, my work for the Lord will never end until Jesus returns, and I stand in the judgment and hear the words, "well done thou good and faithful servant; you have been faithful over a few things; I will make you ruler over many things: Enter thou into the joy of the Lord." St. Matthew 25:23.

With all that I have written in the preceding chapters and what I will write in the final chapter 14, I am led to just allow the photographs, articles, and images in chapter 13 to speak for themselves regarding my retirement. I hope that you will find of particular interest; my retirement celebrations, one given by my wife (a jewel among jewels) at the Hotel Roanoke Conference Center and the second given by the city of Roanoke at the Jefferson Center Atrium. Pictures are worth a thousand words. Seeing is believing.

Fire Chief Announces Retirement Date, New 'Flock' To Tend

Roanoke City Fire Chief Rawleigh W. Quarles, Sr. has announced that he will retire effective March 1, 1995. Quarles, who is a licensed and ordained minister, will focus his efforts on the ministry. He currently serves as the pastor of the Staunton Avenue Church of God.

Quarles has 31 years of service with the Roanoke City Fire Department. He started as a firefighter in 1963, was promoted to lieutenant and became a fire inspector in 1972, followed by a promotion to deputy chief fire marshal in 1977. He became deputy chief of Training in 1987 and was named Roanoke City Fire Chief in 1989.

"Rawleigh Quarles has a significant history of contributions to the city of Roanoke and its citizens," said City Manager Bob Herbert. "We wish him the very best as he pursues his other calling."

Under Quarles direction as fire chief the Fire Department made numerous positive strides including:
• Initiating an equipment replacement program which resulted in the purchase of over $2.25 million worth of vehicles and equipment for the Fire Department. This reduced the average age of department vehicles from 25 years to 15 years.
• Constructed Fire Station #14 in the 460 East corridor to address service needs in that area.
• Introduced the First Responder Program, whereby firefighters at specific stations provide first response to calls for medical assistance until the ambulance arrives. It is now in effect at six stations and has greatly improved response time and service to customers.
• Initiated Officer Leadership Training, ongoing standardized Fire Tower Evolution Training and a customer service program within the Fire Department.
• Began a physical fitness program for all firefighters and hired a new airport training/ health fitness officer.
• To assist in the recruitment of minorities and women in the firefighting profession, introduced a Firefighter Cadet Program whereby high school students get class credit and certification in firefighting skills.

"For over a year, I have devoted my off-work hours to my ministry," said Quarles who became an interim pastor in June 1993, and then was ordained and installed as a full-time pastor in May 1994. "My retirement from the city will allow more time to tend to the needs of my congregation. In many ways, I'm just changing my focus from one flock to another."

Quarles said he decided to announce his retirement now in order to give the city as much advance notice as possible to begin the search for his successor and to help ensure a smooth transition. He added that a new retirement option recently approved by City Council was also an incentive. Under the option, all employees in the city's "old" retirement system will have the option to move into the new retirement system, which in some cases can provide greater benefits.

Rawleigh Quarles
Served five years as fire chief

Roanoke fire chief retires

Quarles to be full-time pastor

By JOEL TURNER
STAFF WRITER

Rawleigh Quarles didn't burn out after five years as Roanoke's fire chief.

But he's taking early retirement because he feels a higher calling — to become a full-time minister so he can better serve his congregation.

"I'm not burned out," he said. "It's just hard trying to wear two hats."

And thanks to a recent change in city policy, he can retire now and receive the same pension as if he had stayed another four years.

Quarles, 52, caught many city officials by surprise Friday when he announced that he will retire March 1.

Quarles, one of the city's first black firefighters and the first black chief, spent most of his adult life climbing through the ranks to get the top job in 1989.

He fought racial discrimination as he moved up the ladder. Quarles won a racial discrimination case against the city when he failed to get the fire marshal's job. He has worked for the city for 31 years, including five years as chief.

Some firefighters who know Quarles' tenacity were surprised that he would give up the post that he battled so hard to get.

But Quarles' love for the chief's job lost out to a deep religious faith and a feeling that it was time to change his profession.

"For over a year, I have devoted my off-work hours to my ministry," Quarles said.

He became interim pastor of the Staunton Avenue Church of God in June 1993. He was ordained earlier this year and has been the full-time

PLEASE SEE **QUARLES**/C5

Quarles

FROM PAGE C1

pastor since May.

"My retirement from the city will allow time to tend to the needs of my congregation. In many ways, I'm just changing my focus from one flock to another," he said.

City Manager Bob Herbert said Quarles has made significant contributions to the city during three decades. "We wish him the very best as he pursues his other calling."

Quarles said he wouldn't have retired for another four years if City Council had not allowed employees to transfer from the city's old retirement plan to a new one. In some cases, this enables employees to receive higher benefits.

Quarles has been embroiled in several controversies during his years with the city.

The most recent occurred three years ago when there were allegations that he had misused state funds, rigged bids on fire trucks and accepted improper gratuities from a fire-engine company.

State police spent three months investigating the allegations, but no charges were placed.

Commonwealth's Attorney Don Caldwell said Quarles had shown poor judgment, but there was no evidence to support criminal charges.

In an interview then, Quarles said he harbored no ill feelings and did not want to rehash the investigation.

It was prompted by a group of firefighters who sent a letter to the state attorney general listing the allegations against him.

He said the controversy was not a factor in his decision to retire now.

Quarles began his career as firefighter in 1963 and became a fire inspector in 1972. He was named fire marshal and deputy chief in 1977 after the U.S. Equal Employment Opportunity Commission ruled that he had been denied the job because he is black.

Quarles was appointed deputy chief for training in 1987 and became chief two years later.

The Fire Department has made several changes in recent years that have been credited to his leadership. They include:

■ Initiating an equipment replacement program to replace old fire trucks. This reduced the average age of fire trucks from 25 to 15 years.

■ Building Fire Station No. 14 on Orange Avenue in the Northeast community.

■ Introducing a first-responder program so firefighters in six fire houses can answer calls for medical assistance.

■ Beginning a physical fitness program for all firefighters.

■ Initiating leadership training for officers and a customer service program in the department.

Quarles has a reputation for being a chief who tried to project a professional image for himself and the Fire Department. Quarles wears the chief's uniform whenever he attends City Council meetings or other public events.

Fire chief Quarles retires in Roanoke

After serving the city for 31 years, **Rawleigh Quarles** will retire as Roanoke's fire chief March 1.

Quarles, one of the city's first black firefighters and the first black chief, began his career as firefighter in 1963 and became a fire inspector in 1972. He was named fire marshal and deputy chief in 1977. Quarles was appointed deputy chief for training in 1987 and became chief two years later.

In June 1993, Quarles became interim pastor of the Staunton Avenue Church of God. This past year, he was ordained and has been full-time pastor since May.

"My retirement from the city will allow time to tend to the needs of my congregation. In many ways, I'm just changing my focus from one flock to another," he said.

The Roanoke Tribune

Making and Recording Black History Since 1939

ROANOKE, VIRGINIA, THURSDAY, APRIL 13, 1995

VOLUME LVI -- NUMBER 51

Publication No. (USPS 646-080)

30¢

Retirement Banquet Held for Roanoke's First Black Fire Chief

It was an historic occasion in many ways when the family of the Rev. Raleigh W. Quarles, Sr. honored him at an elegant dinner in recognition of his retirement from the City of Roanoke as Fire Chief. The grand affair was held Saturday evening at the newly renovated, revitalized and re-opened Hotel Roanoke where some 375 family members and guests were in attendance.

Rev. Charles T. Green, president of the local chapter NAACP, served as the gracious Master of Ceremony, masterfully directing some 28 speakers and performers listed on the program through the evening of accolades, reminiscence and entertainment which included the presentation of awards and expressions of love, admiration and highest respect.

The battery of program participants, which began with a former school teacher and neighbor, Ms. Sarah Saunders, included city officials Bob Herbert, Skip Stead, City Councilwoman, Elizabeth Bowles; Roanoke City Deputy Fire Chief Winston Simmons and District Fire Chief Thomas R. Tyne. Other firefighting associations were represented by: Roscoe T. Hagar, international Association of Black Professional Firefighters (IABPFF), Fairfax County, VA; Fire Chief Julian A. Taliaferro, director, Southern Division of the International Association of Fire Chiefs (IAFC), Charlottesville; Fire Captain Francine Aureh, chairperson, Equal Employment Opportunity/Affirmative Action Council, Virginia Office of Fire Training Programs, Hampton, and Fire Chief Stephen P. Kopczynski, vice chairman Virginia Fire Services Board, Charlottesville.

Local ministers participating on the program at the head table included Dr. K. B. Wright, Rev. W. L. Lee, Rev. Pauline Haskins, former Mayor Dr. Noel C. Taylor and Rev. Tommy Lonson Investigators Award for "Distinguished Service Representing the Association as a member of the Virginia Fire Services Board."

The first musical selection was appropriately performed by the multi-talented Nicole Quarles, daughter of the honoree; followed respectively with solos by the gracious Christine Payne and Elsie Scott, with Roma Turner rendering a most impressive performance of the "Creation."

Lynwood R. Welcher, a former classmate, and Ms. Nancy M. Guilliod, sister of the honoree, also added to the evening's indelible memoirs before the final remarks were heard from the most grateful honoree who gave highest praise to his wife for her constant support through his 31 years of service with the city, the last 5-1/2 of which were as Fire Chief.

Prestigious recognitions and awards to the exalted honoree included:

* International Association of Black Professional Firefighters award for "Dedication in Ministering and Directing the City of Roanoke Virginia Fire and Emergency Services."

* International Association of Arson Investigators Award for "Distinguished Service Representing the Association as a member of the Virginia Fire Services Board."

* A resolution from the Department of Fire Programs, Virginia Fire Services Board and the Equal Employment/Affirmative Action Council for his service as a liaison of the Fire Services Board to the EEO/AA Council.

* A resolution from the Department of Fire Programs and the Virginia Fire Services Board for his service as a Fire Services Board Member.

* A proclamation from the Office of the Mayor of the City of Roanoke in recognition of outstanding contributions and accomplishments, and proclaiming Saturday, April 8, 1995 as Raleigh W. Quarles, Sr. Day.

* A United States flag given by Congressional Fire Service members and flown over the United States Capitol on February 10, at the request of the Honorable Thomas J. Biley, Jr., member of Congress. This flag was flown on the occasion of his completion of the National Fire Academy's Executive Fire Officer's Program.

* A Certificate of Completion from the Congressional Fire Service Institute for his successful completion of the Executive Fire Officer's Program.

The evening's event was climaxed with Rev. Quarles presenting a dozen long stem red roses and reading a tribute to his wife for her 33 years of support, dedication and love and for being the greatest wife God has given to man.

RALEIGH W. QUARLES, SR.

Pictures of the City of Roanoke Retirement Dinner Held at the Jefferson Center Atrium

*The City of Roanoke
welcomes you to a*

Retirement Reception

honoring

Rawleigh W. Quarles, Sr.
Fire Chief, City of Roanoke

Friday, February 24, 1995

*Jefferson Center Atrium
2:00 p.m. - 4:00 p.m.*

*"Salute to the men in gear,
professionals who confront
unequalled peril
with unsurpassed courage."*

PROGRAM

Welcome & Introductions

George C. Snead
Public Safety Director, City of Roanoke

Invocation

James D. Ritchie
Assistant City Manager

Presentations

Billy W. Southall
Deputy Fire Chief

George C. Snead
Public Safety Director, City of Roanoke

W. Robert Herbert
Roanoke City Manager

David A. Bowers
Mayor, City of Roanoke

Remarks

Rawleigh W. Quarles, Sr.
Fire Chief

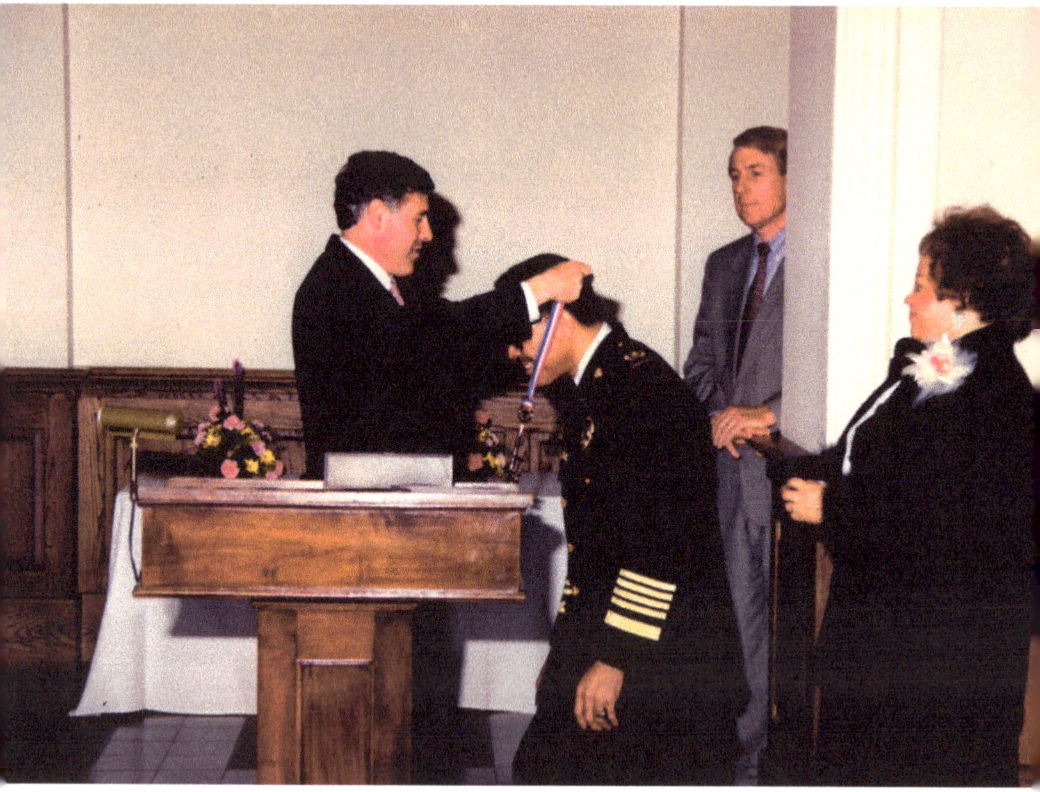

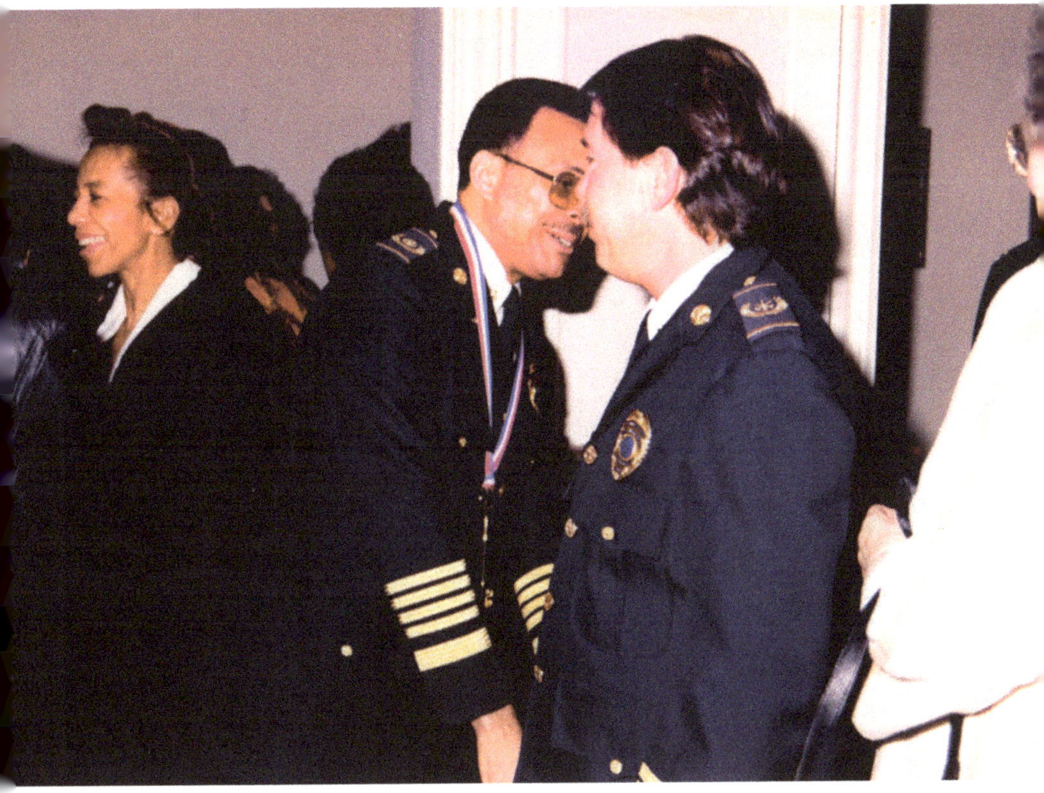

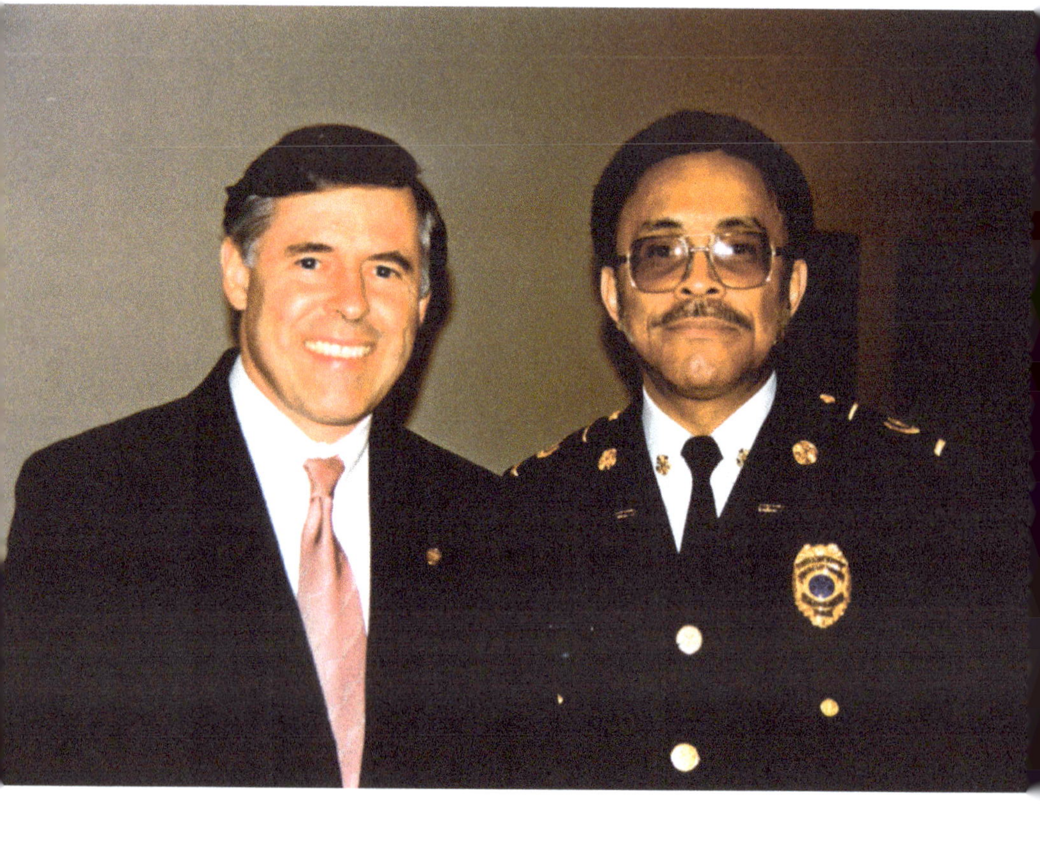

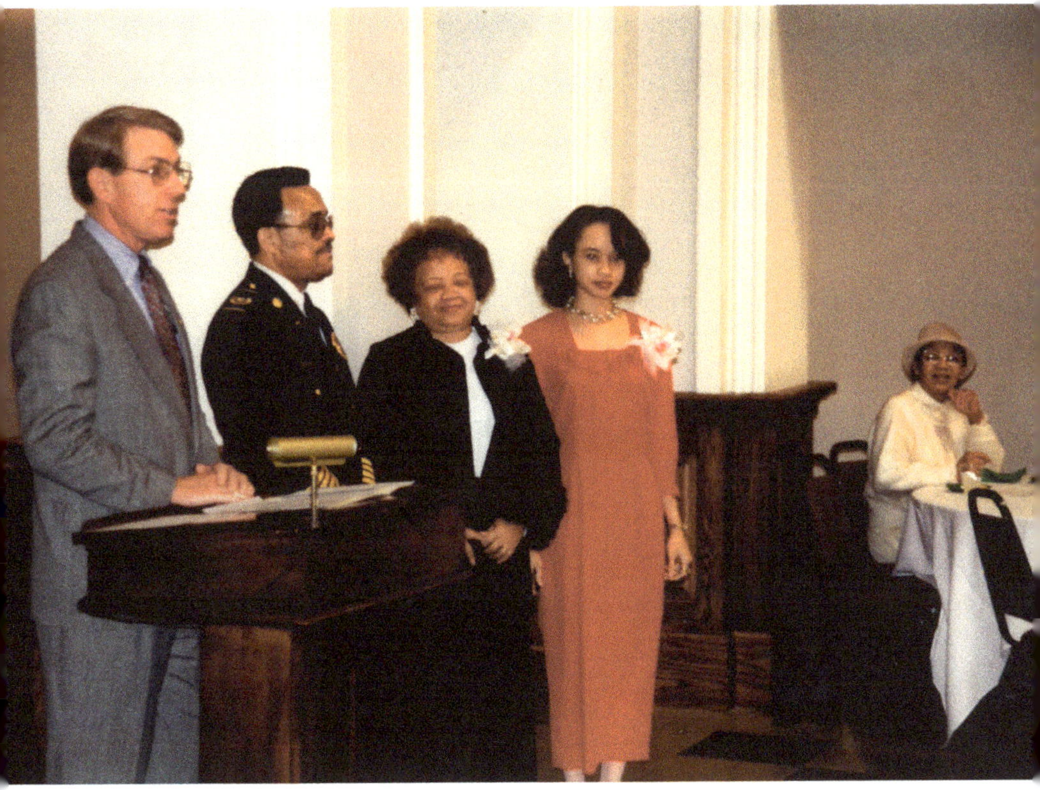

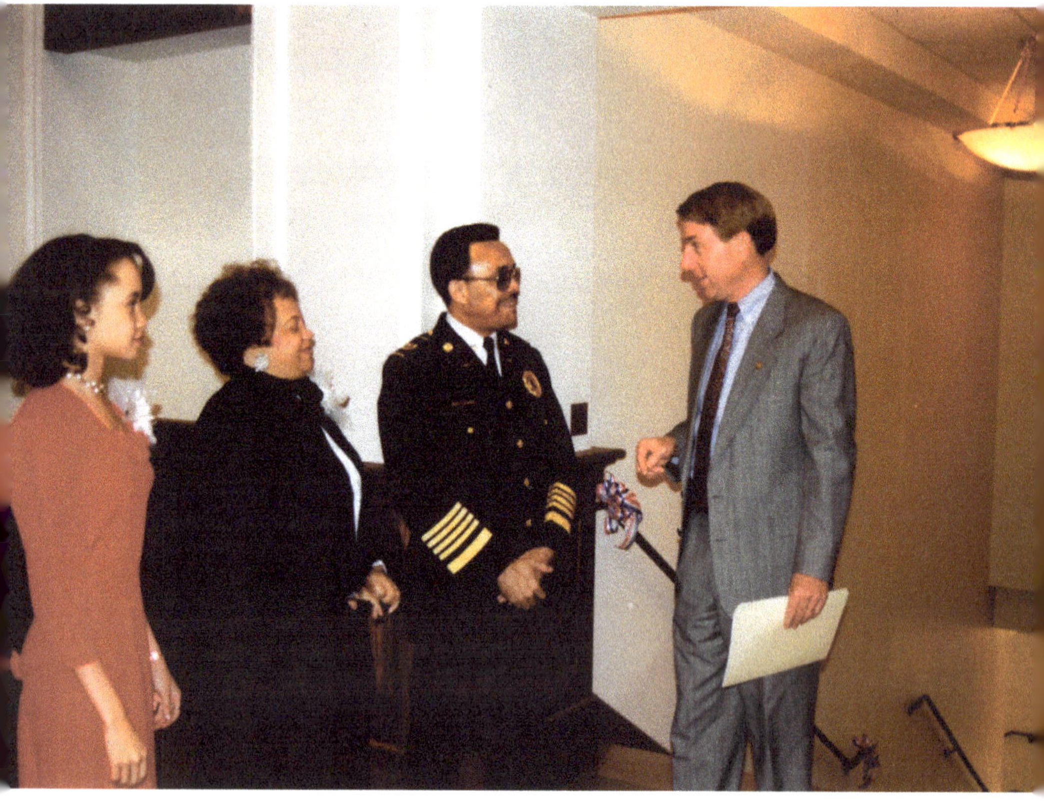

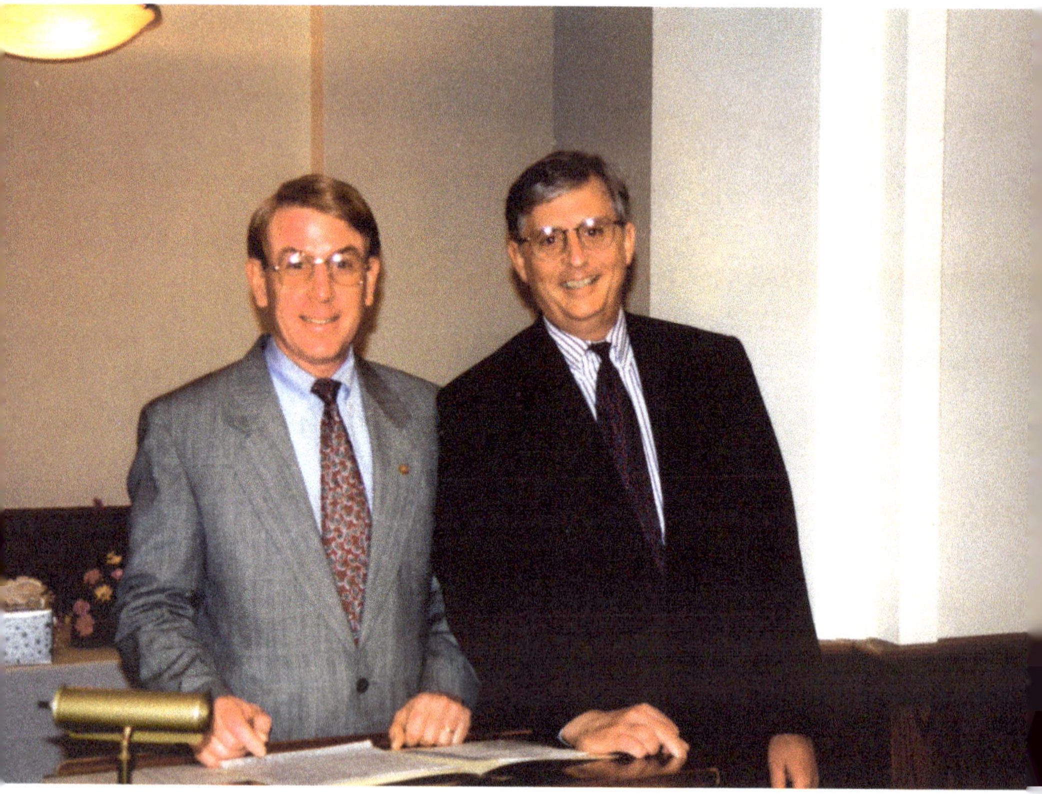

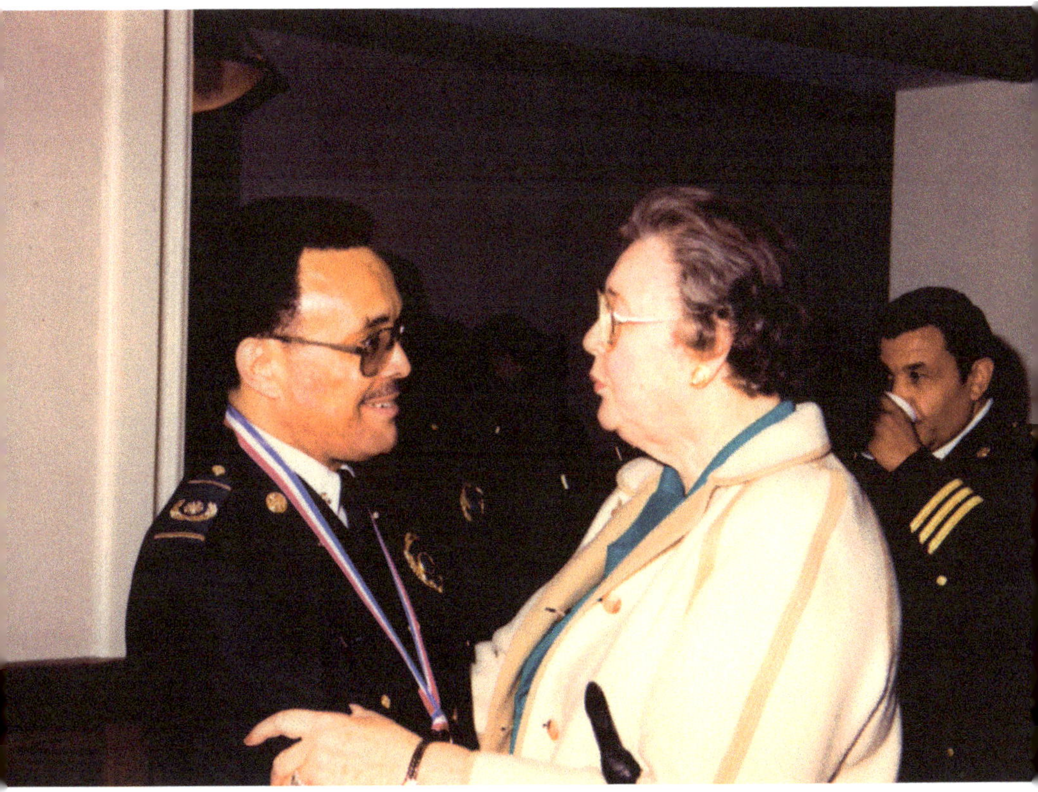

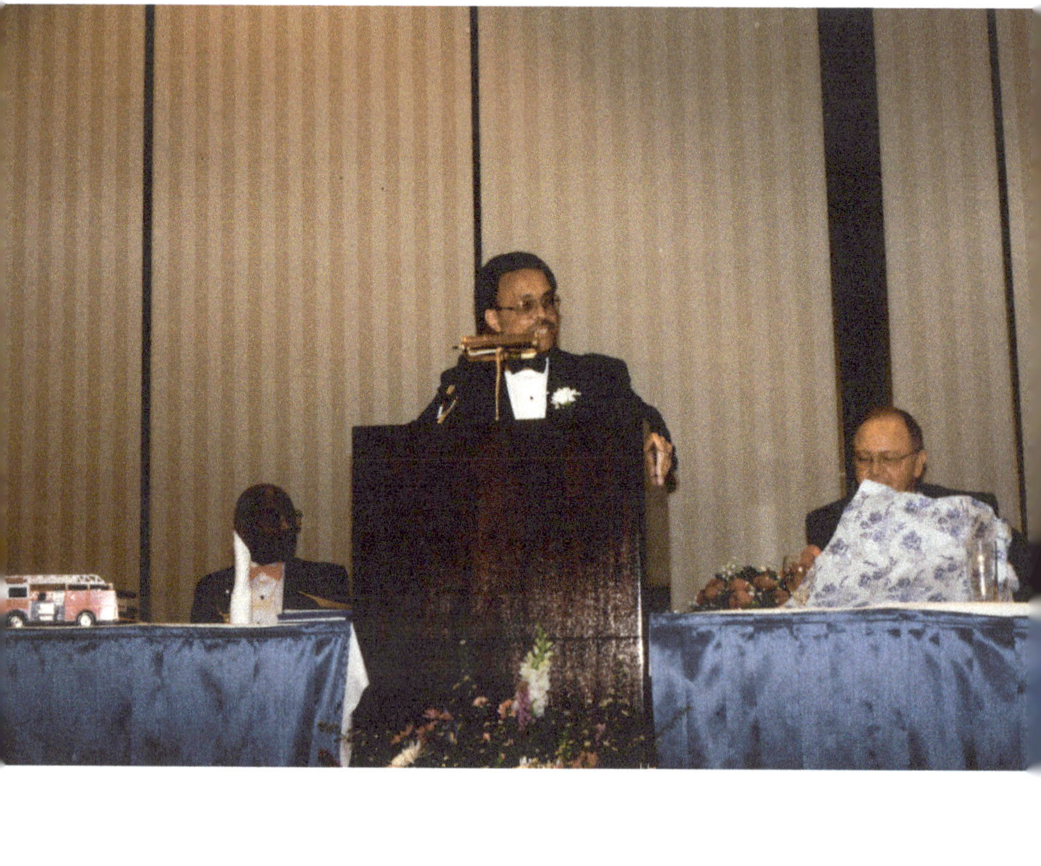

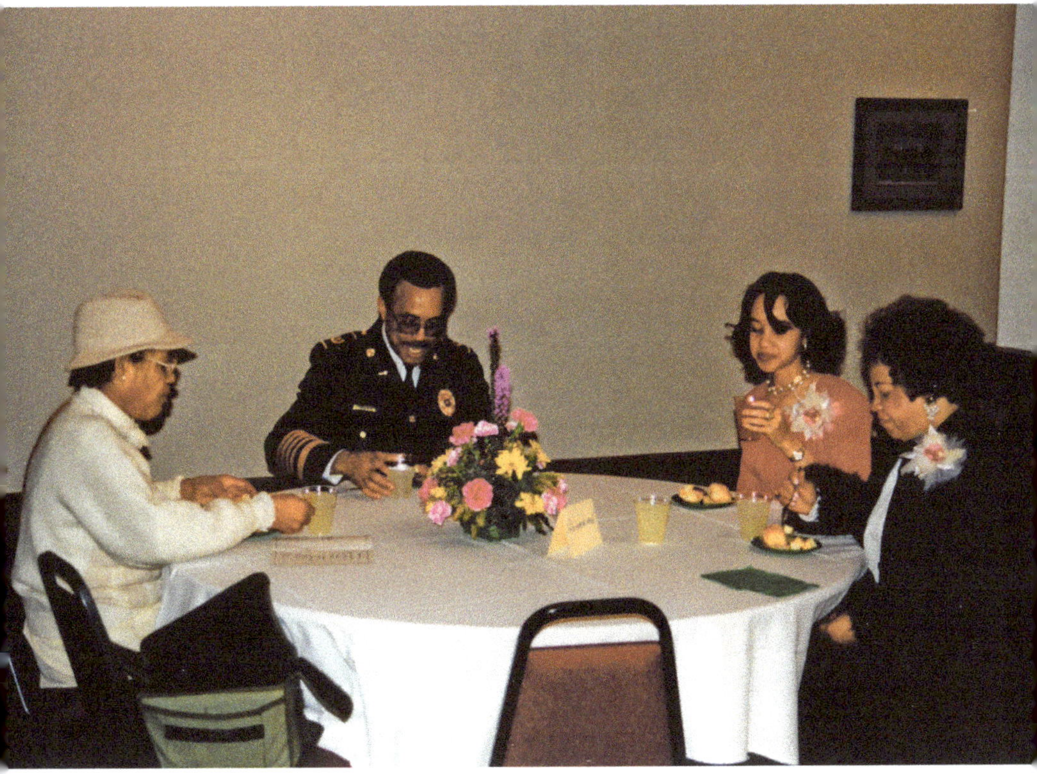

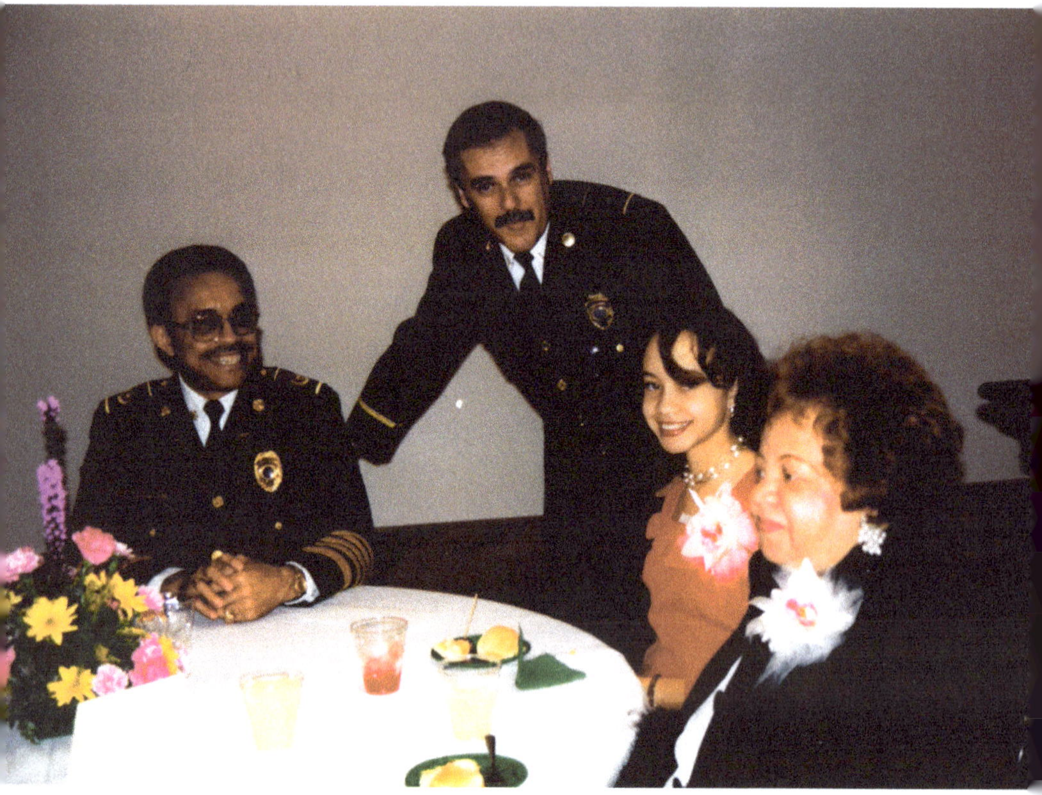

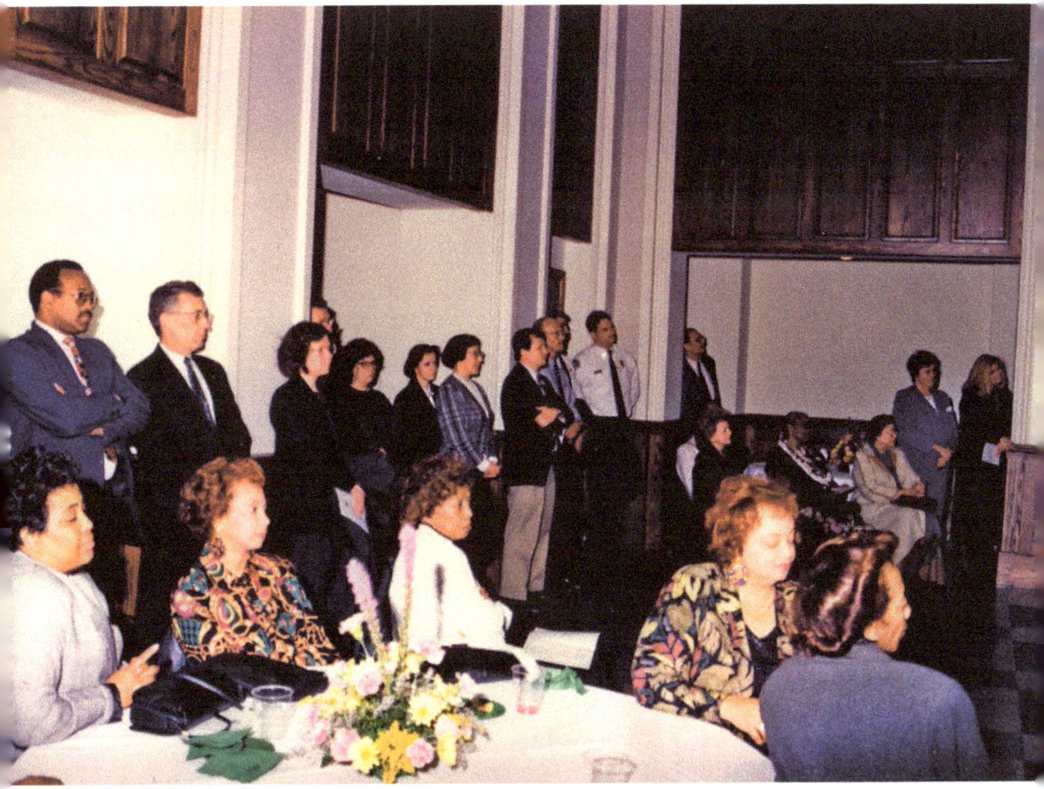

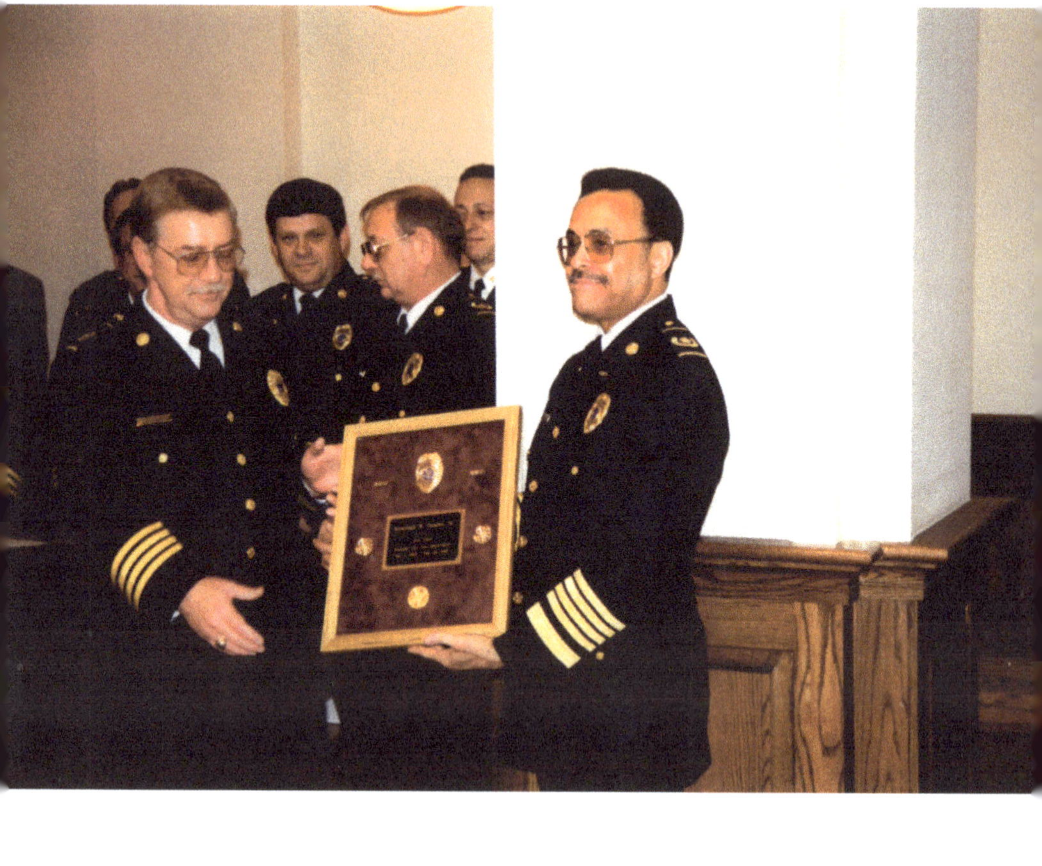

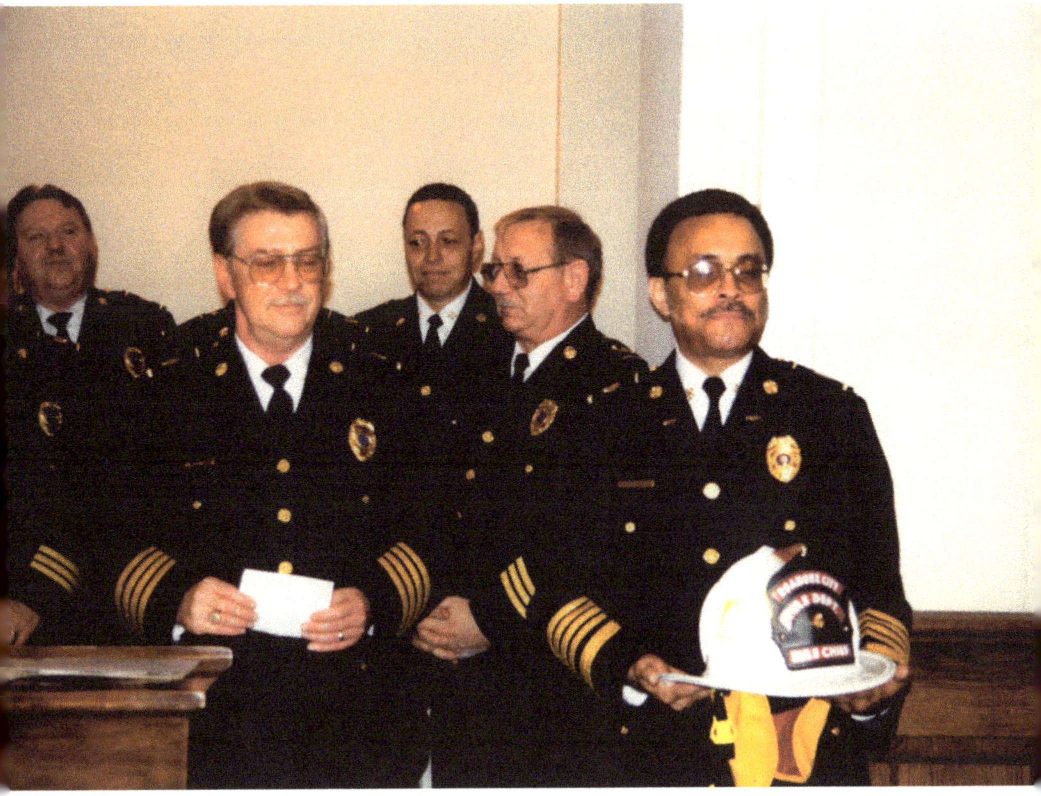

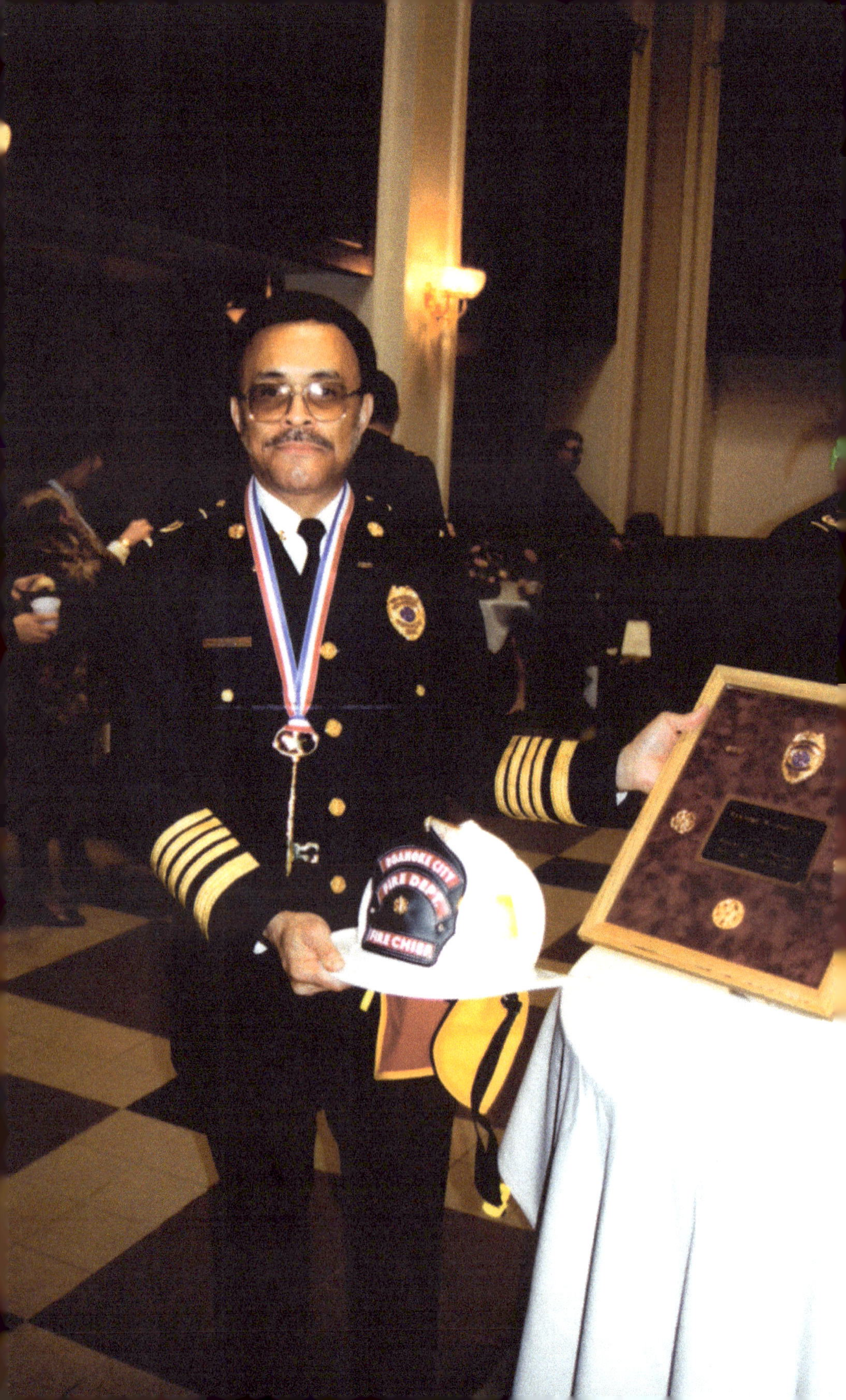
ROANOKE CITY
FIRE DEPT.
FIRE CHIEF

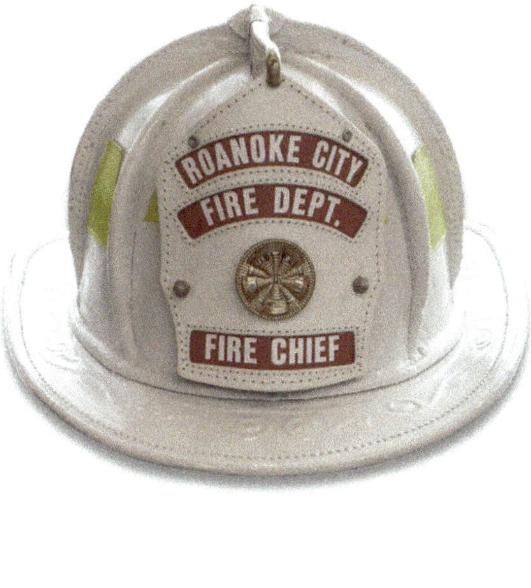
ROANOKE CITY
FIRE DEPT.
FIRE CHIEF

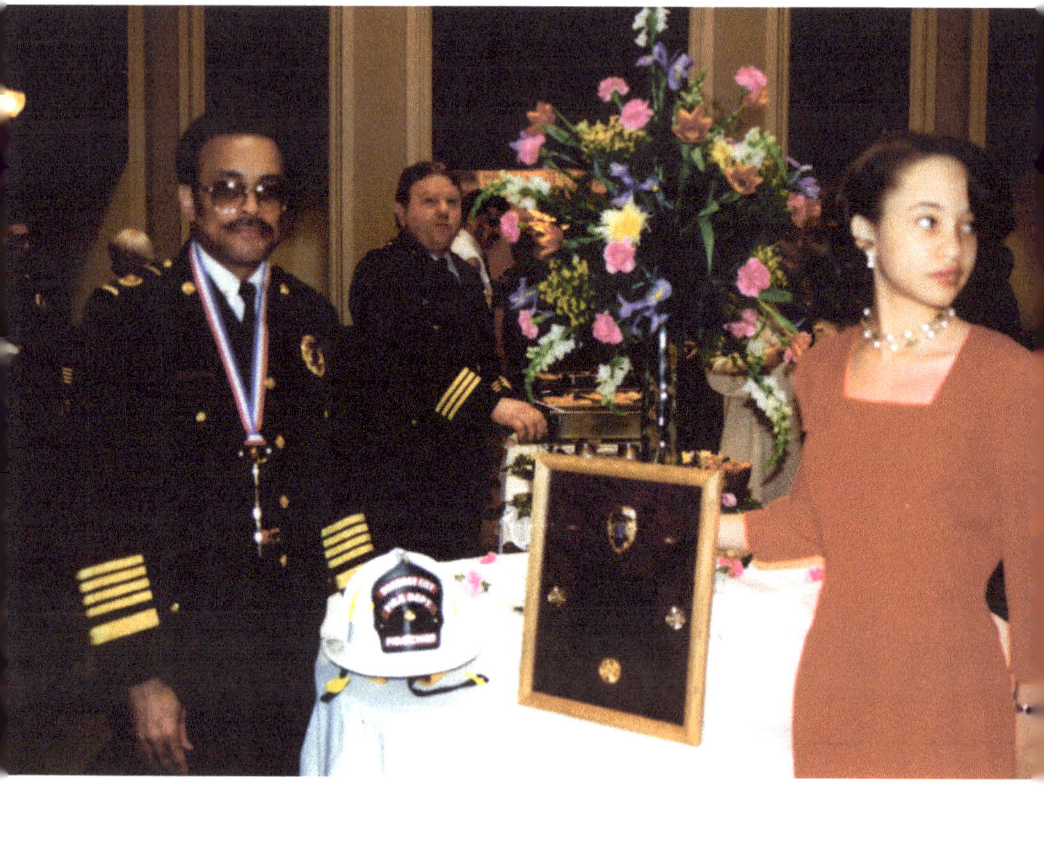

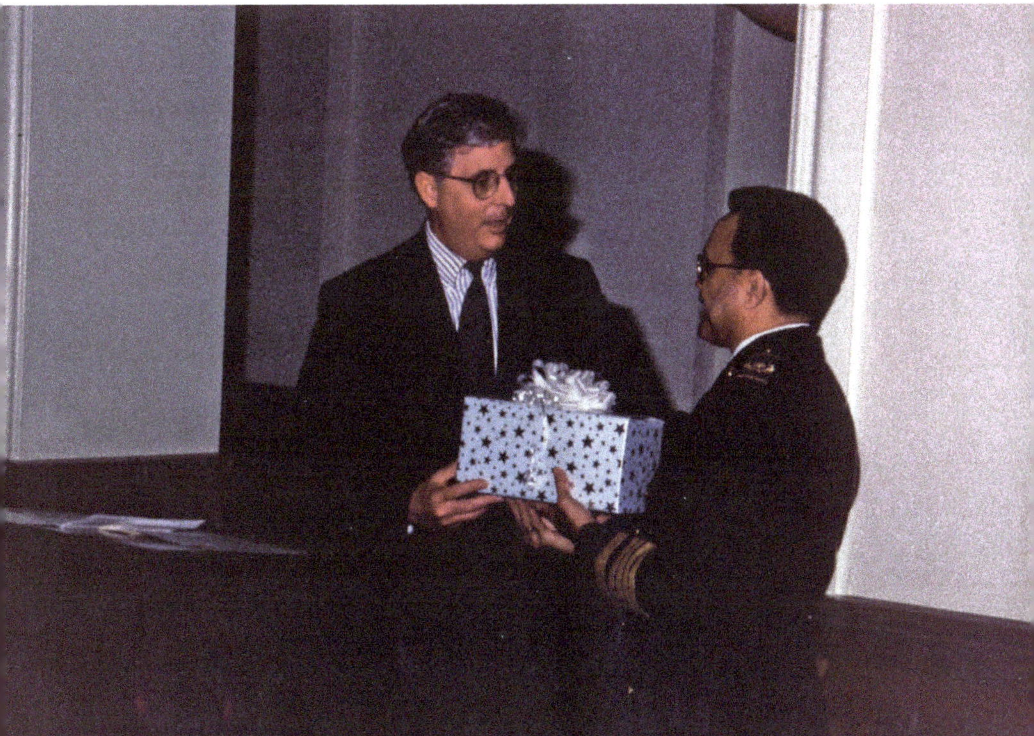

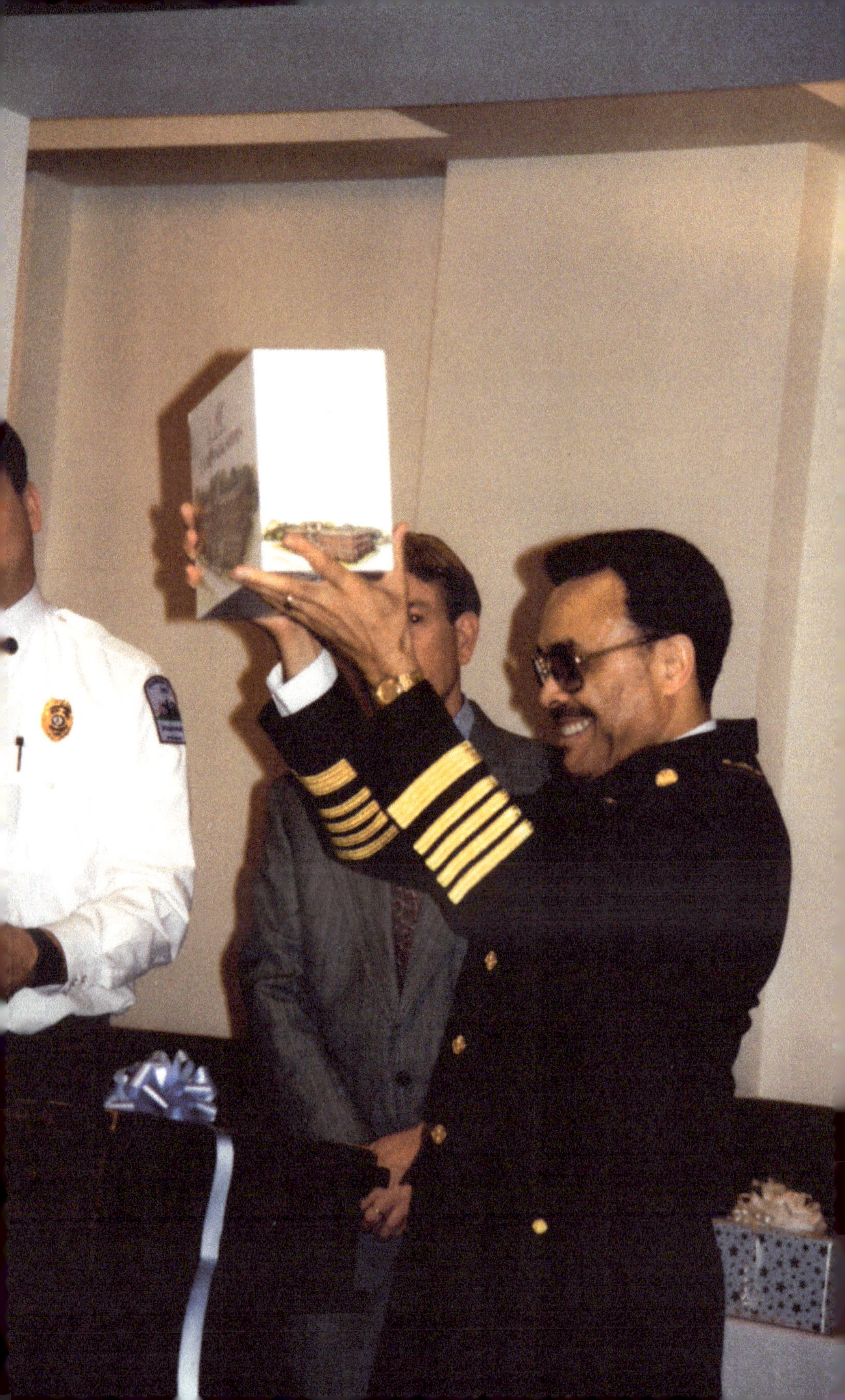

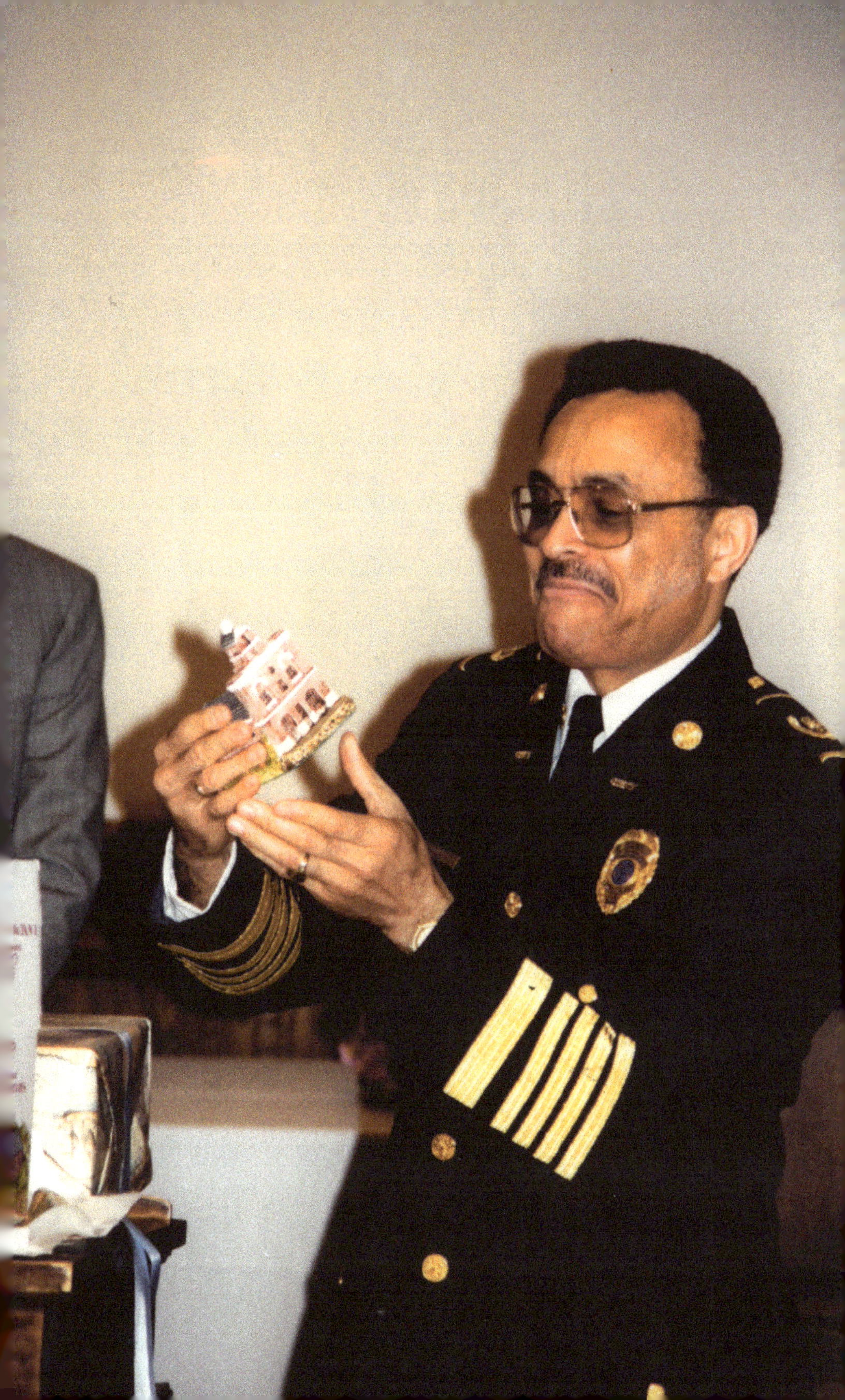

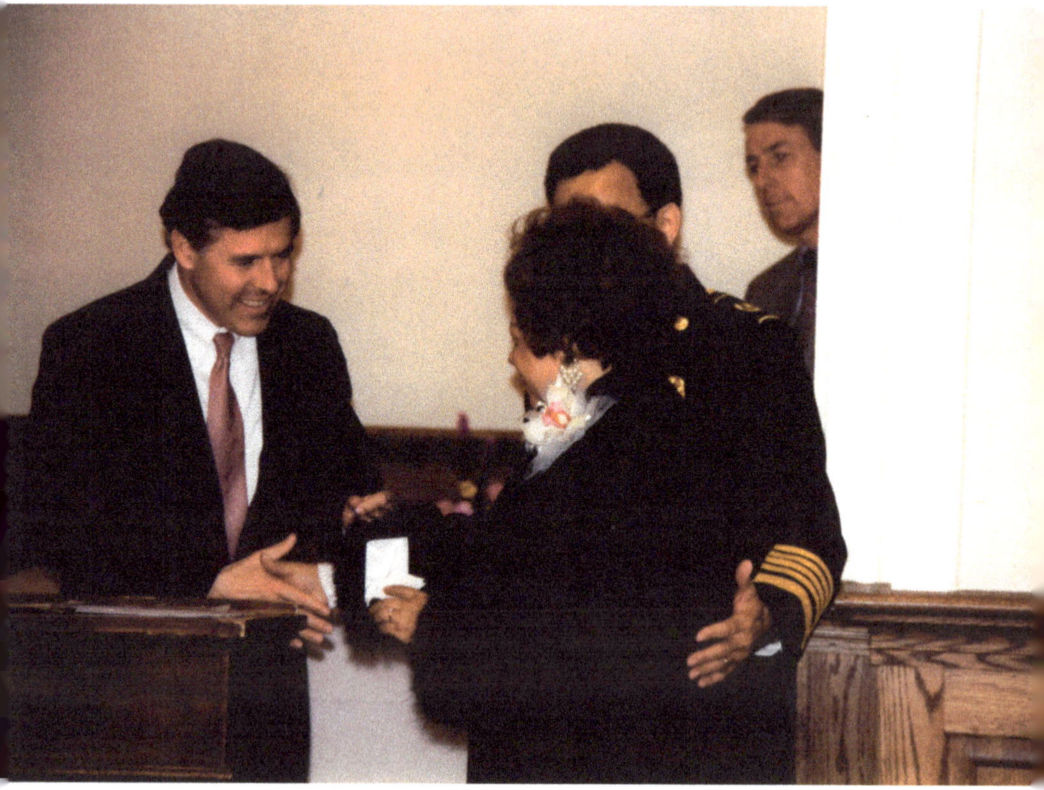

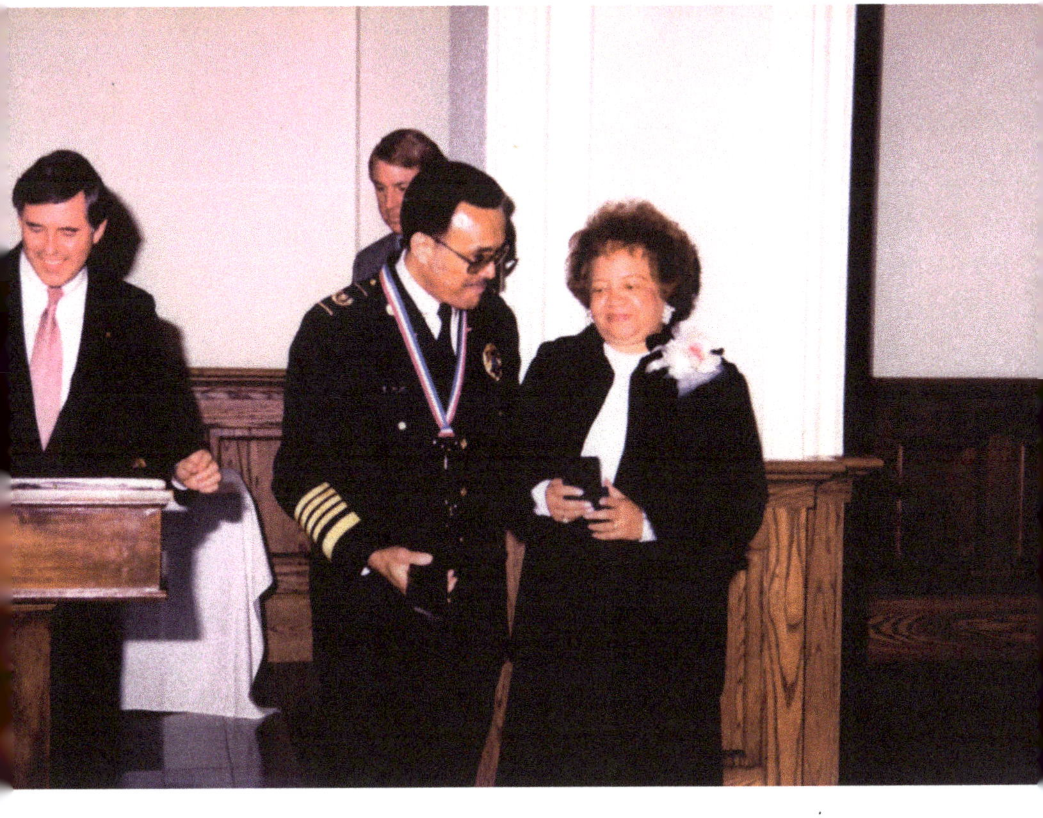

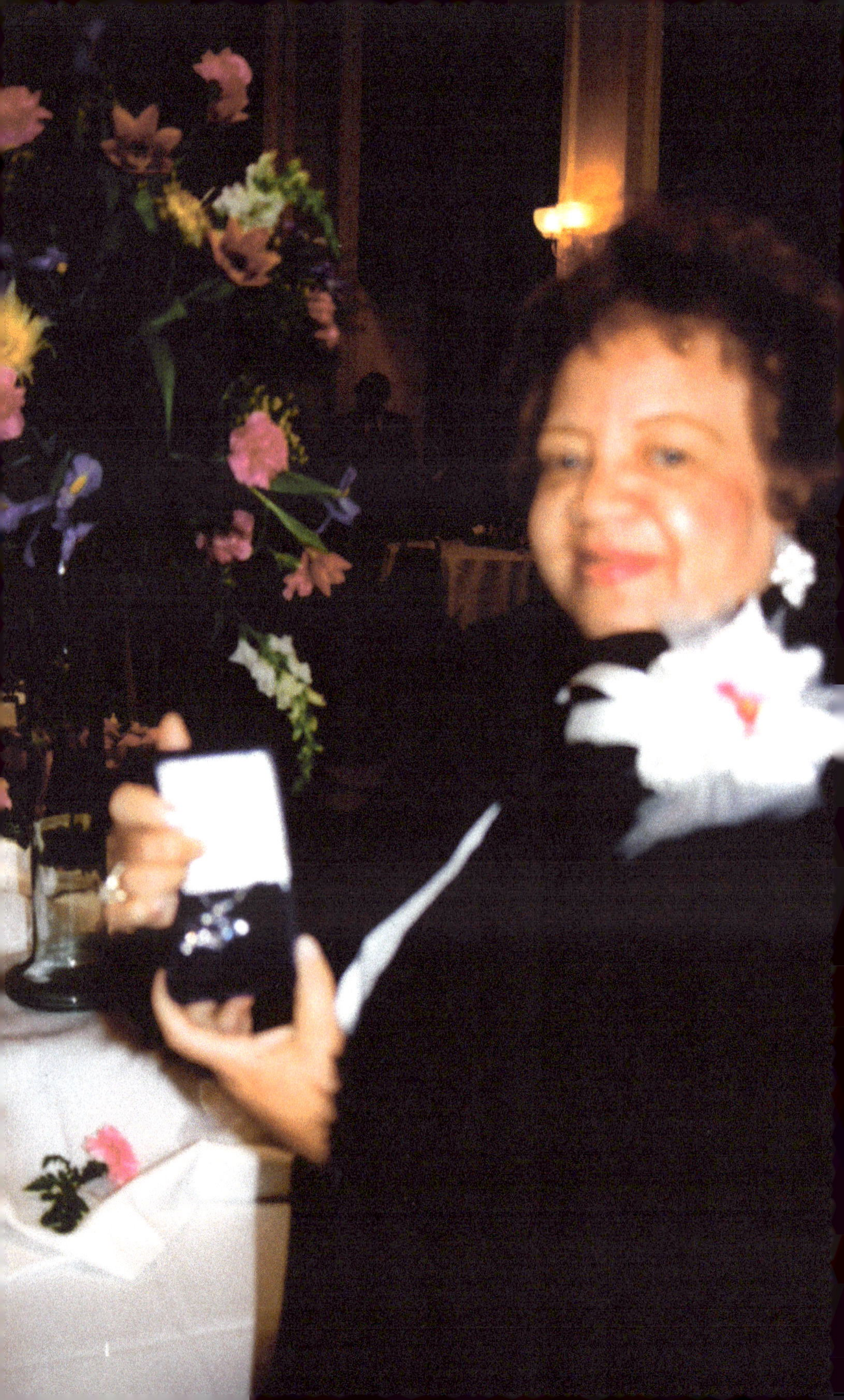

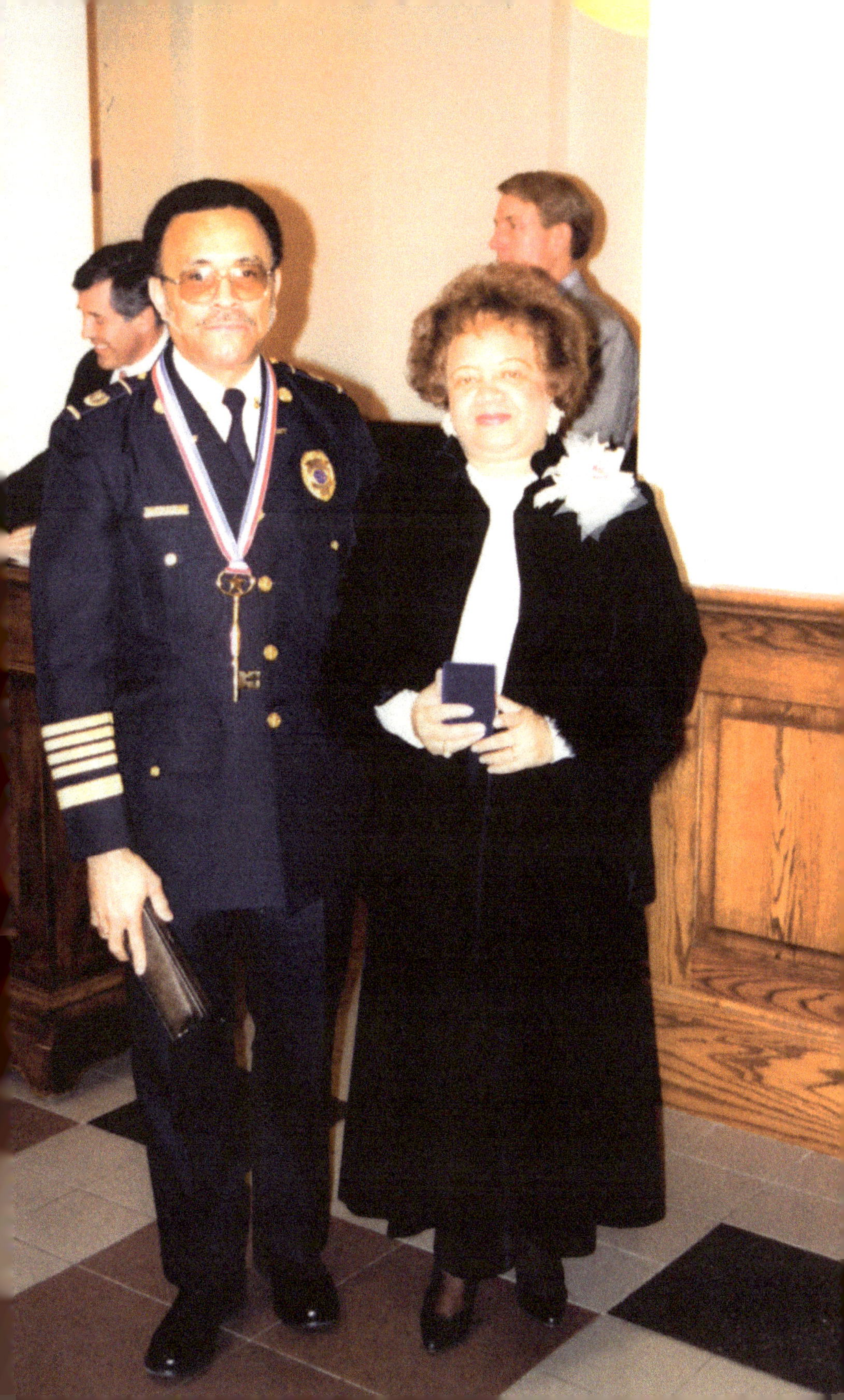

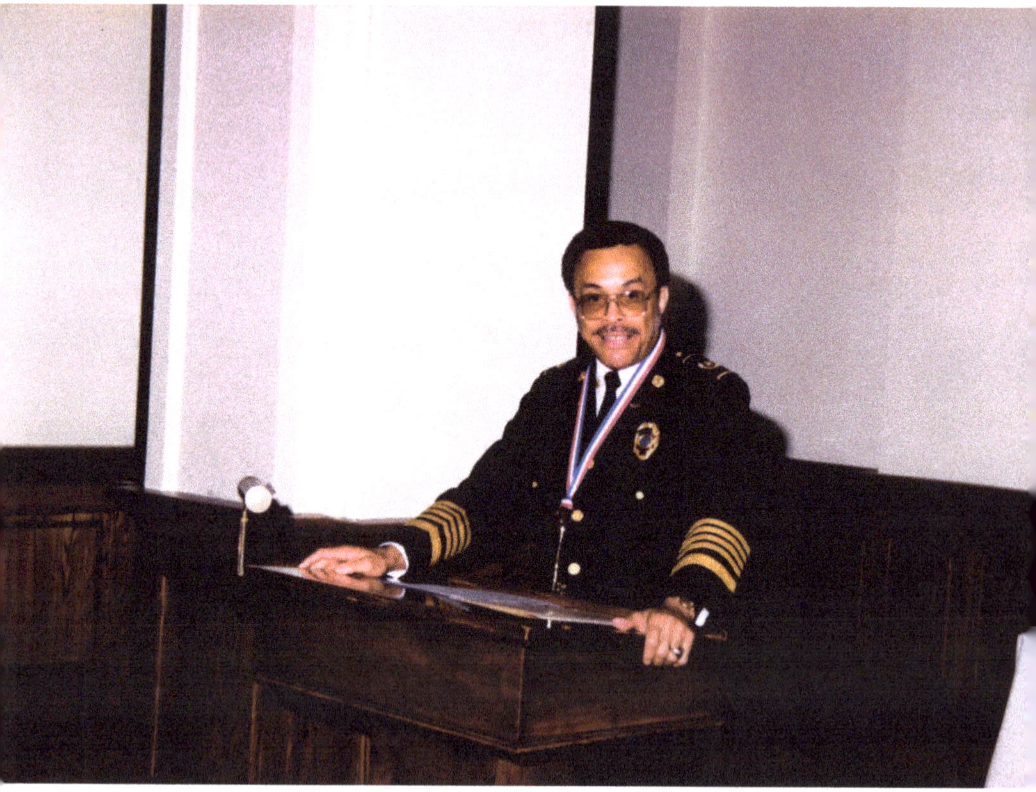

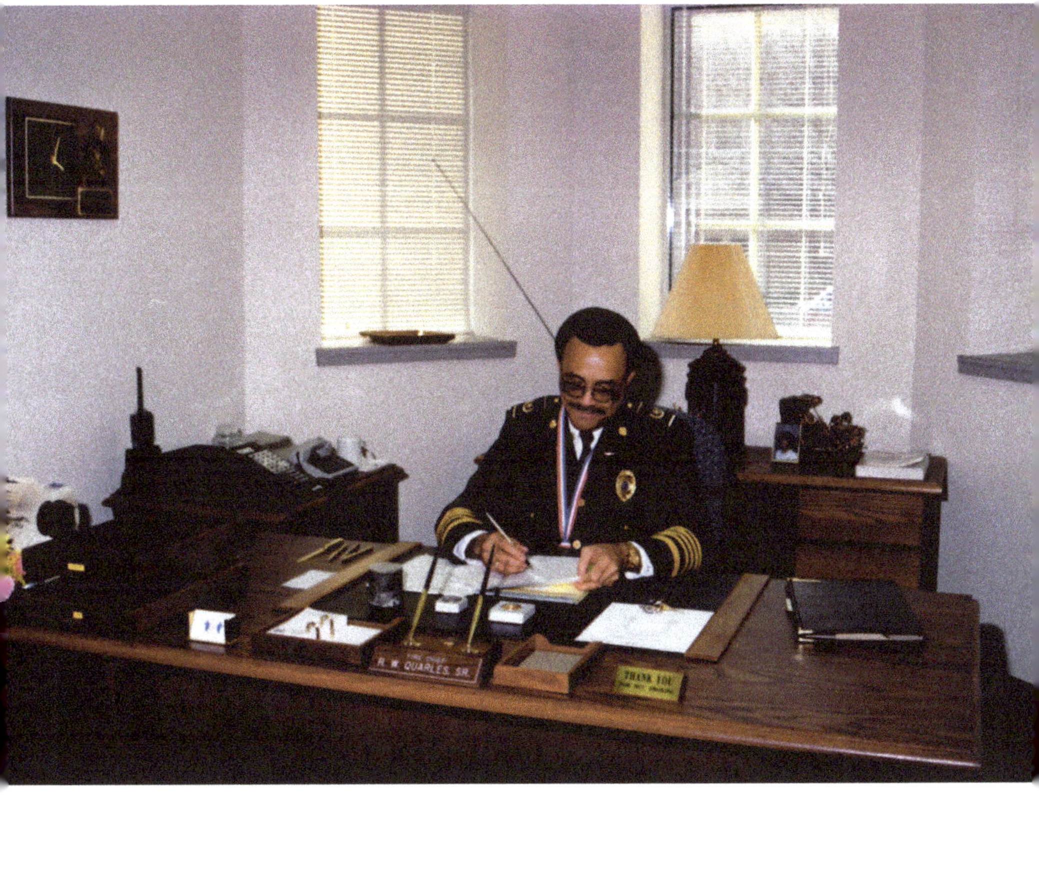
R. W. QUARLES, SR.
THANK YOU

ACKNOWLEDGEMENTS

A Special Thank You To:

Mrs. Mary Parker, City Clerk
Mrs. Gayle Clingenpeel, Floral Arrangements
Murphy's Catering Service

Pictures of Retirement Dinner Given by my wife Barbara at the Hotel Roanoke and Conference Center

THE QUARLES FAMILY

welcomes you to a

RETIREMENT DINNER

honoring

RAWLEIGH W. QUARLES, SR.
Fire Chief, City of Roanoke (Retired)

Saturday, April 8, 1995
6:30 p.m. - 9:30 p.m.

The Hotel Roanoke and Conference Center
110 Shenandoah Avenue
Roanoke, Virginia 24016

PROGRAMME

Welcome .... **Reverend Charles T. Green**
President, Nat'l Association for Advancement of Colored People (NAACP)

Invocation .... **Reverend Charles C. Briscoe**
Pastor, First Church of God, Salem VA

- DINNER -

Tribute .... **Sarah S. Saunders**
Former School Teacher

Remarks .... **W. Robert Herbert**
Roanoke City Manager

Remarks .... **George C. Snead**
Director of Public Safety, Roanoke City

Remarks .... **Reverend Kenneth B. Wright**
Pastor, First Baptist Church, Roanoke, VA

Instrumental Solo .... **Nicole Y. Quarles**

Remarks .... **Bobby L. Stanley**
Acting Director, Department of Fire Programs, Richmond, VA

Remarks .... **Reverend William L. Lee**
Pastor, Loudon Avenue Christian Church, Roanoke, VA

Remarks .... **Reverend Noel C. Taylor**
Pastor, High Street Baptist Church, Roanoke, VA

Remarks .... **Reverend Pauline Haskins**
Associate Minister, Staunton Avenue Church of God and Minister at Large

Remarks .... **Lynwood R. Welcher**
Former Classmate

Solo .... **Christine K. Payne**

Remarks .... **Roscoe T. Hagar**
Fire Sergeant; Virginia Representative for The International Association of Black Professional Firefighters (IABPFF), Fairfax County, VA

PROGRAMME
(continued)

Remarks .... **Marilyn L. Curtis**
Vice Chairman, Roanoke City School Board; Representative of Business Community

Remarks .... **Nancy M. Guilliod**
Sister of Honoree

Remarks .... **Winston V. Simmons**
Deputy Fire Chief, Roanoke City Fire Department

Remarks .... **Julian A. Taliaferro**
Fire Chief; Director, Southeastern Division of International Association of Fire Chiefs (IAFC), Charlottesville, VA

Duet .... **Reverend and Mrs. Tommy London**

Presentation .... **Thomas R. Tyree**
District Fire Chief, Roanoke City Fire Department

Presentation .... **Elizabeth T. Bowles**
Roanoke City Council

Presentation .... **Francine Auroda**
Fire Captain; Chairperson, Equal Employment Opportunity/Affirmative Action Council, Virginia Office of Fire Training Programs, Hampton, VA

Presentation .... **James W. O'Rourke**
Fire Marshal; President, Virginia Chapter International Association of Arson Investigators (IAAI), Fairfax County, VA

Presentation .... **Stephen P. Kopczynski**
Fire Chief; Second Vice President State Fire Chiefs' Association of Virginia (SFCAV), York County, VA

Presentation .... **Julian A. Taliaferro**
Fire Chief; Vice Chairman, Virginia Fire Services Board, Charlottesville, VA

"Creation" .... **Roma C. Turner**

Solo .... **Elsie C. Scott**

Remarks .... **Reverend Rawleigh W. Quarles, Sr.**
Honoree

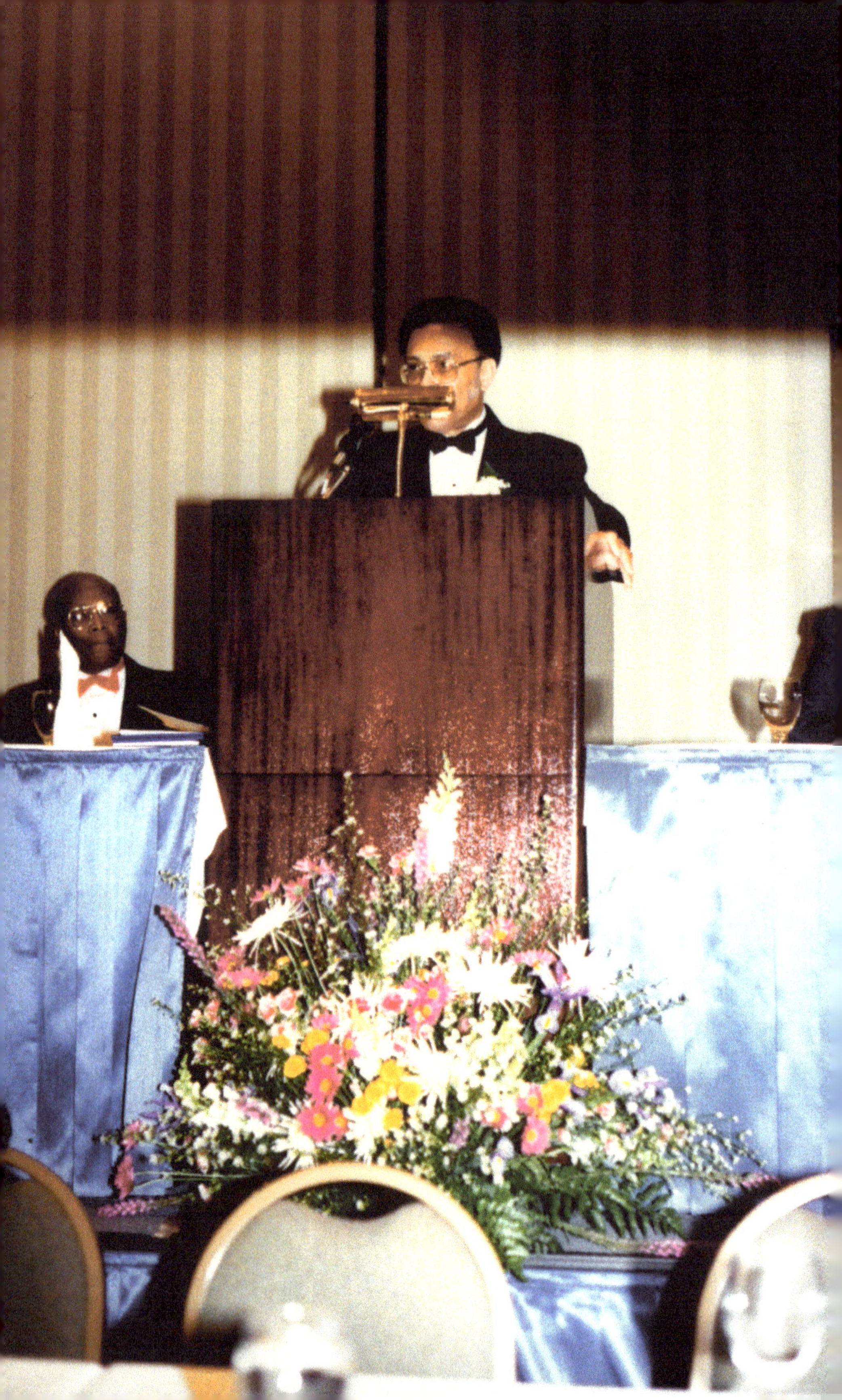

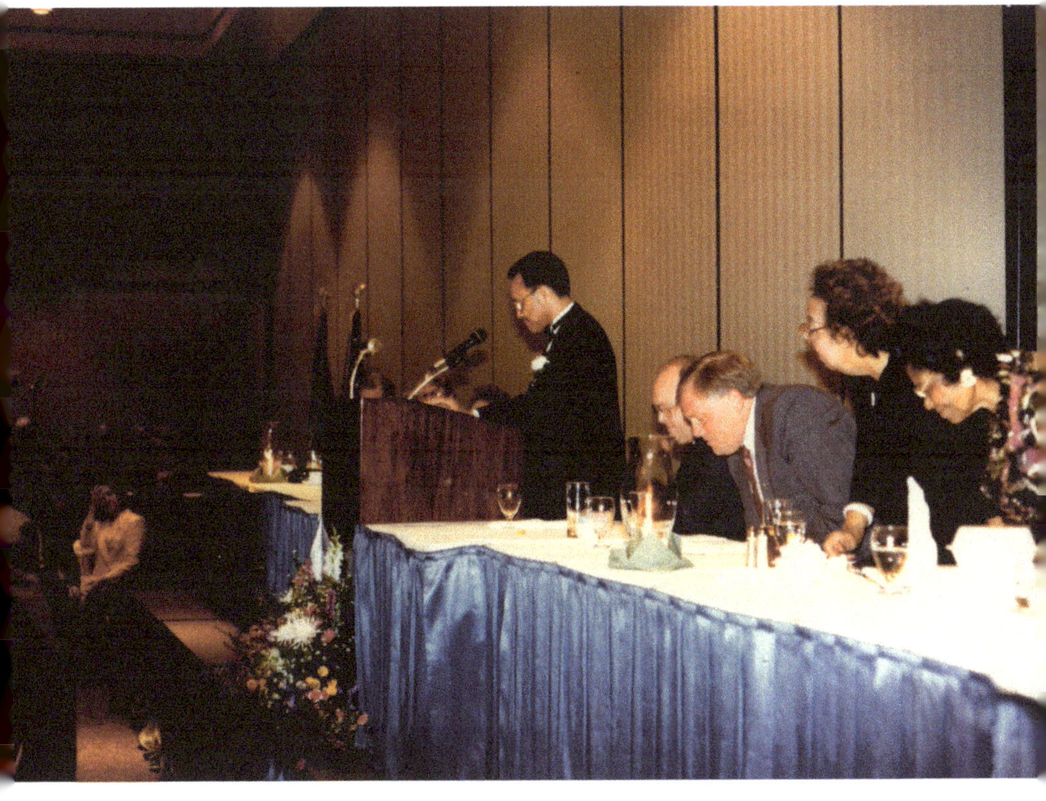

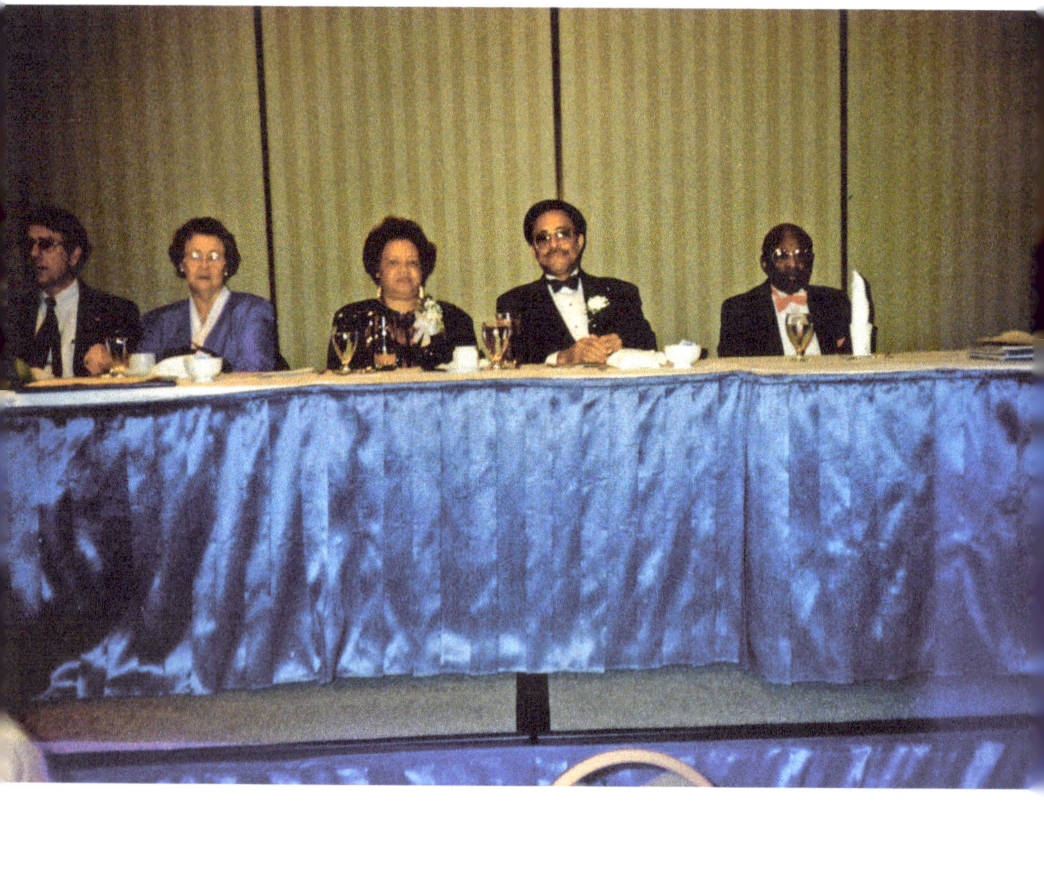

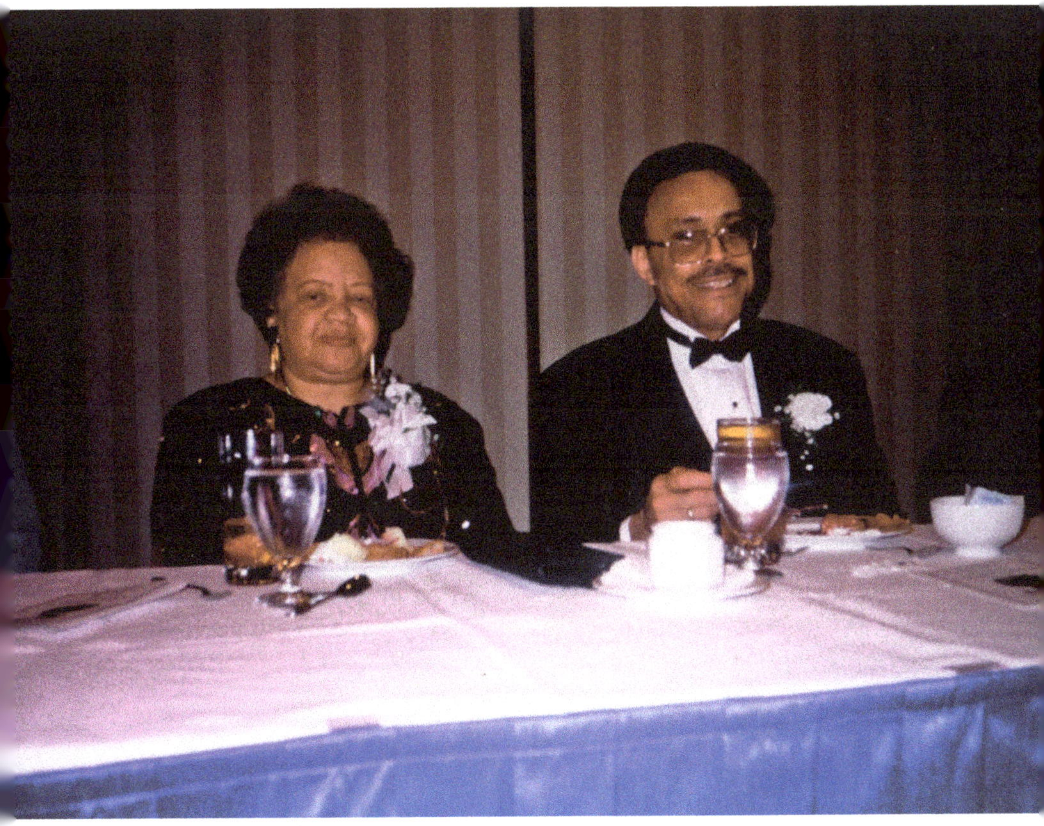

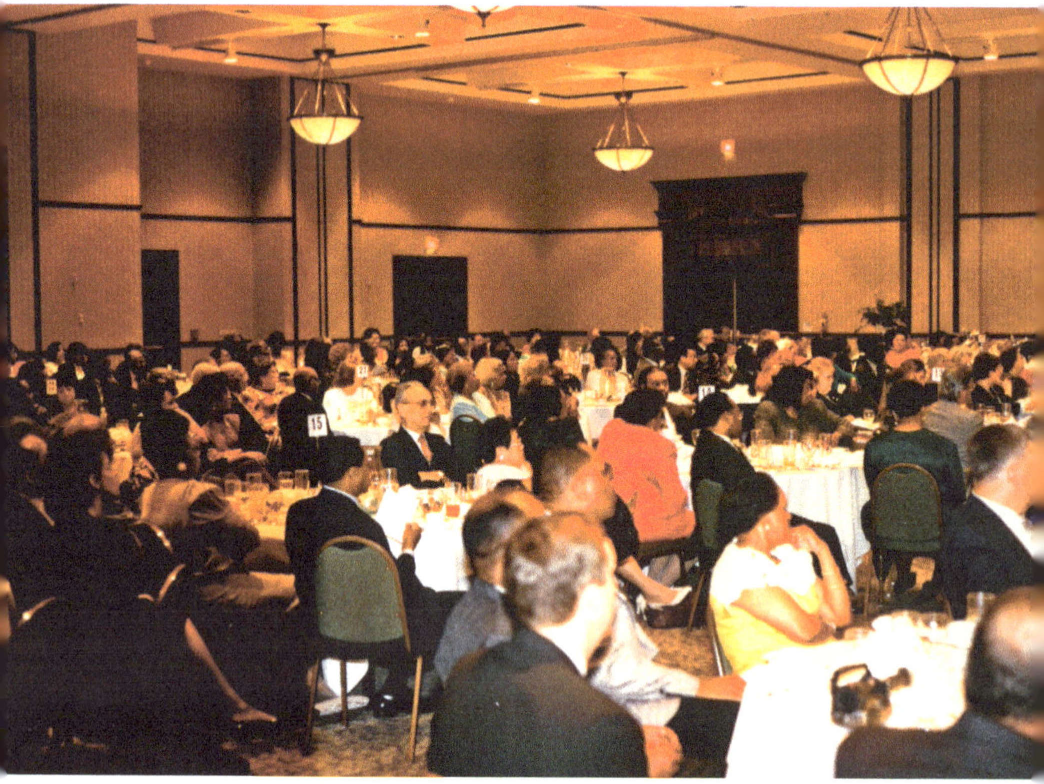

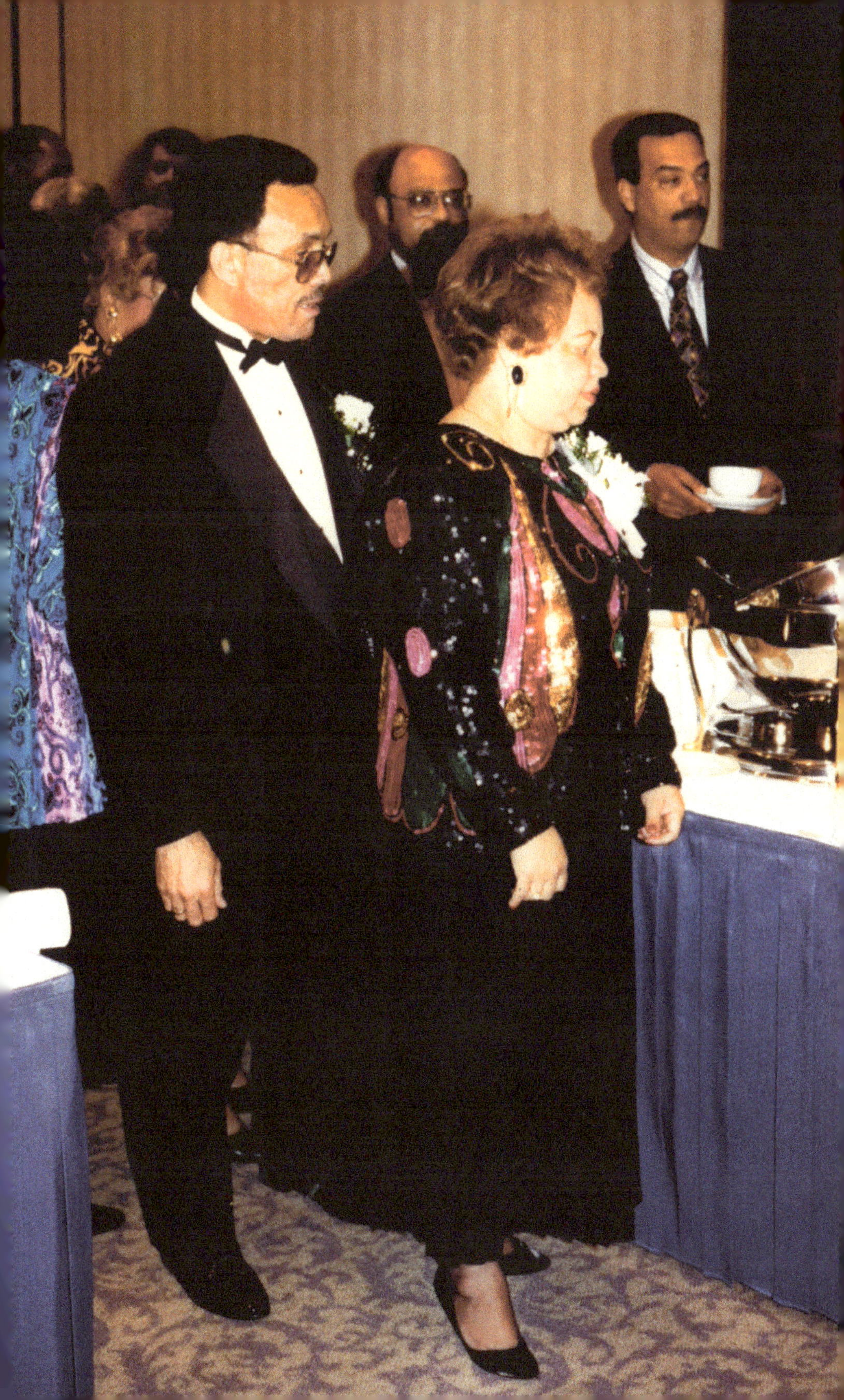

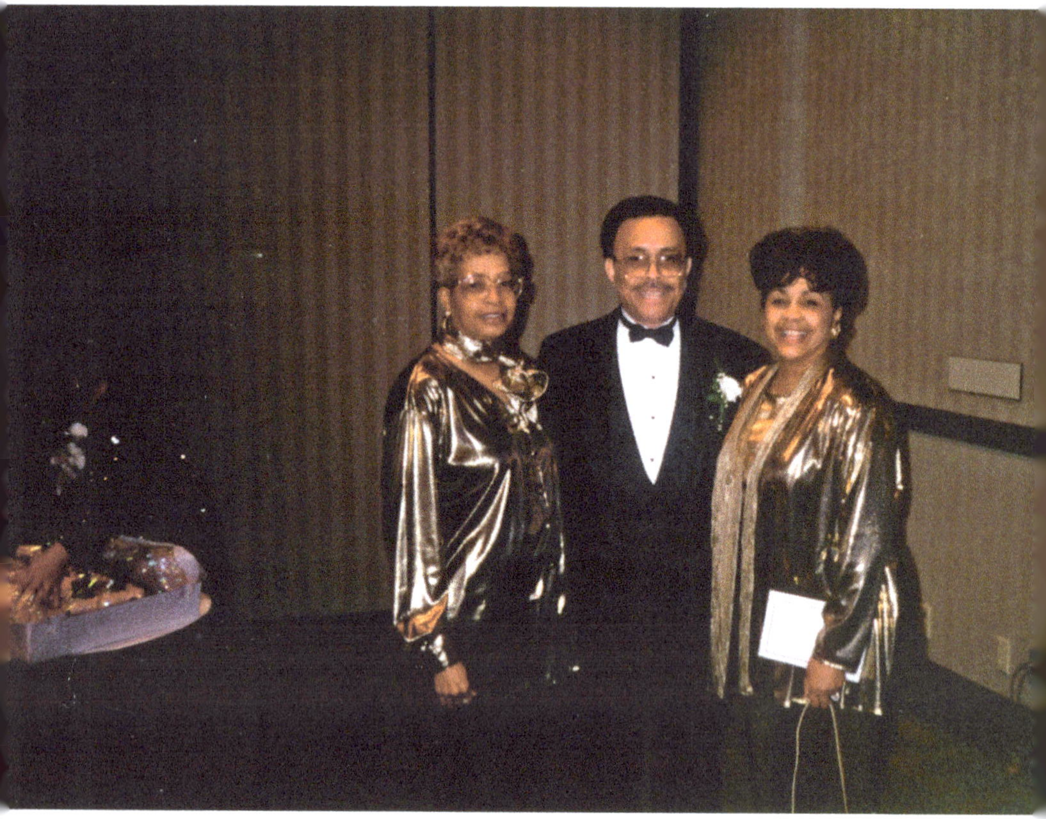

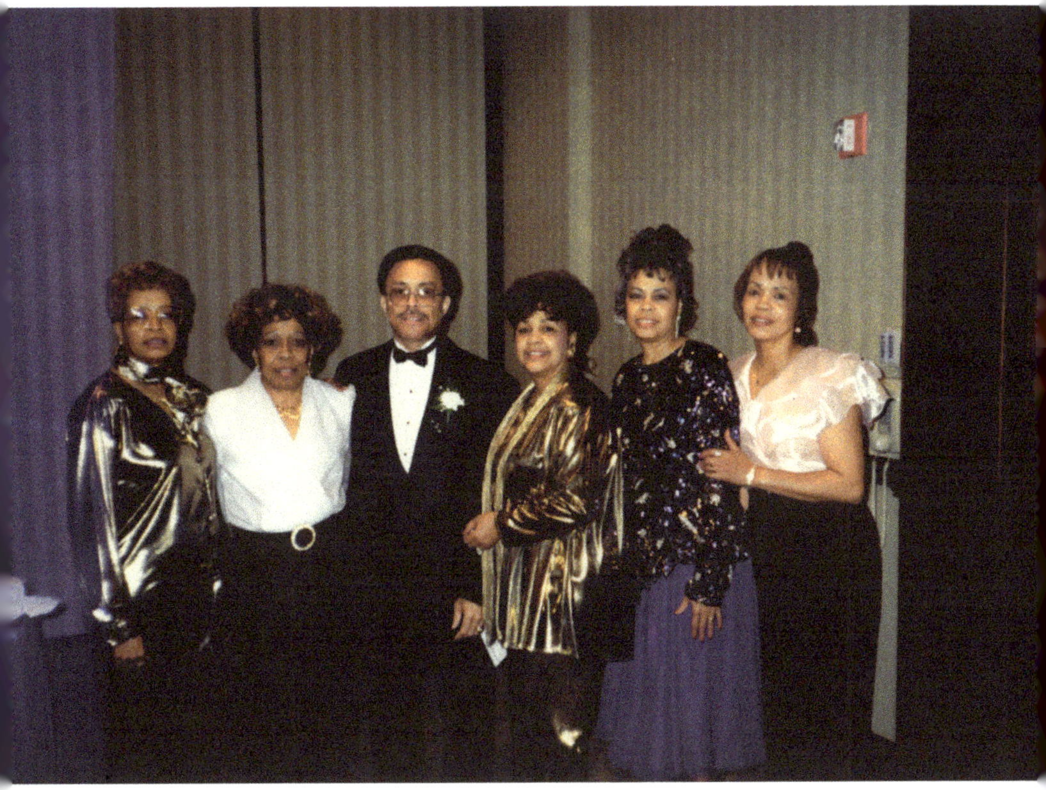

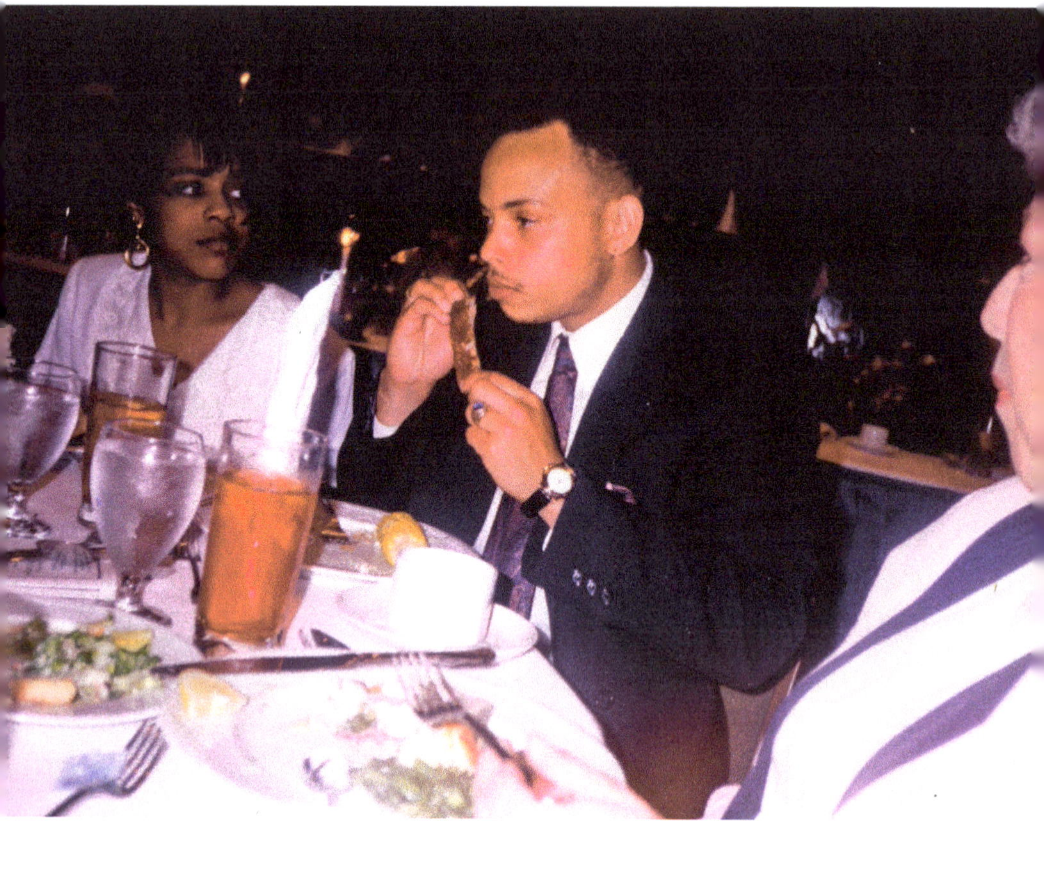

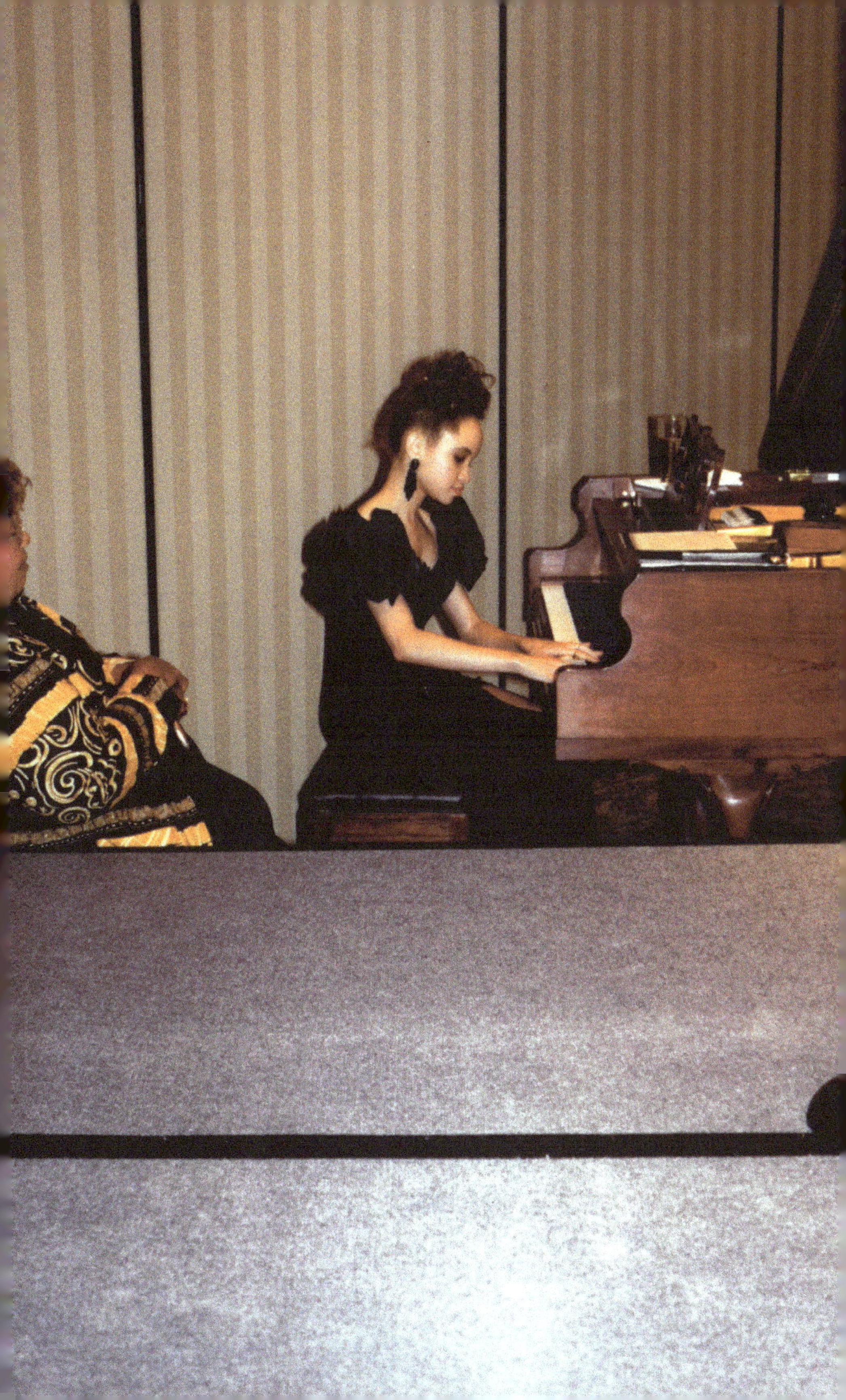

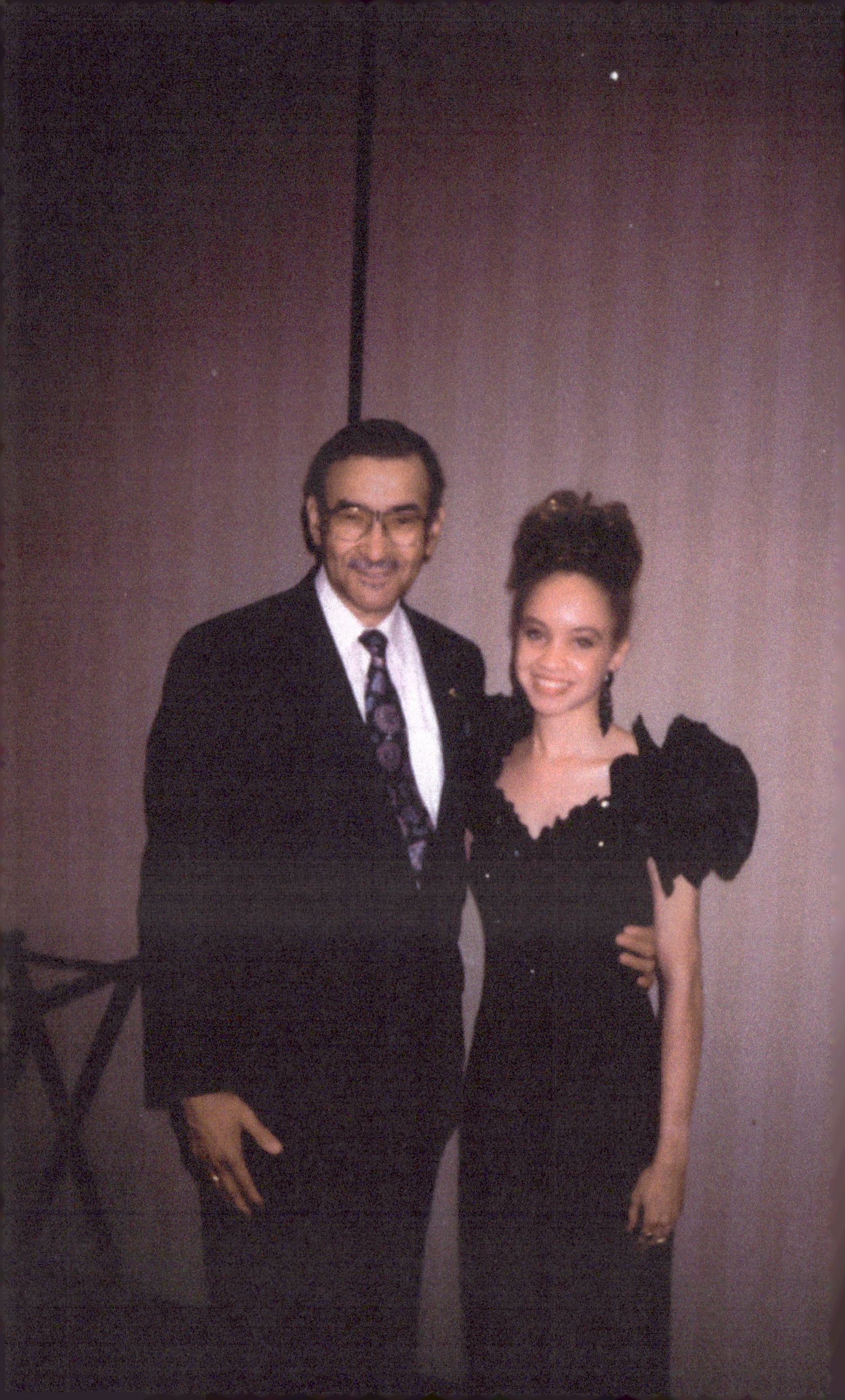

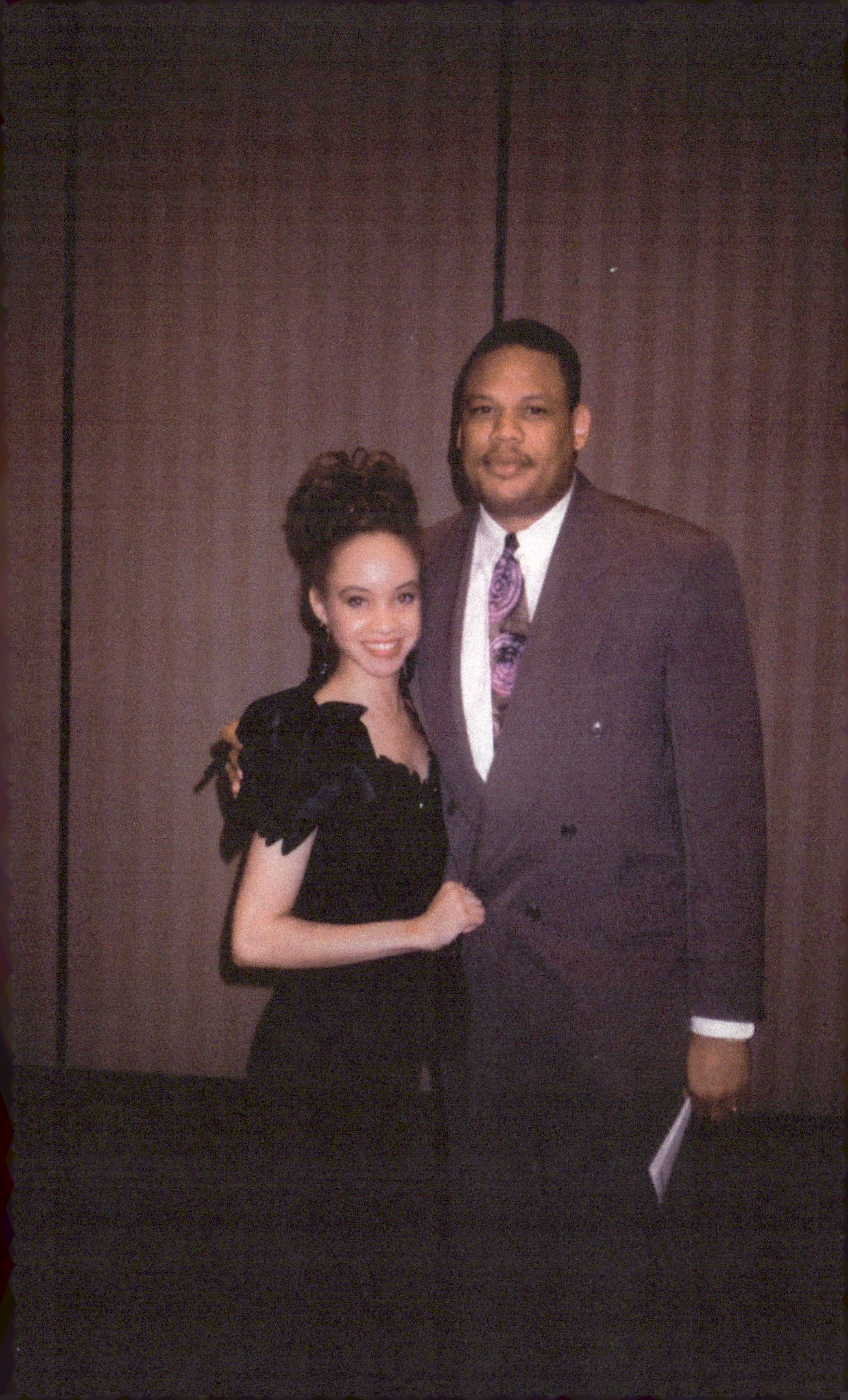

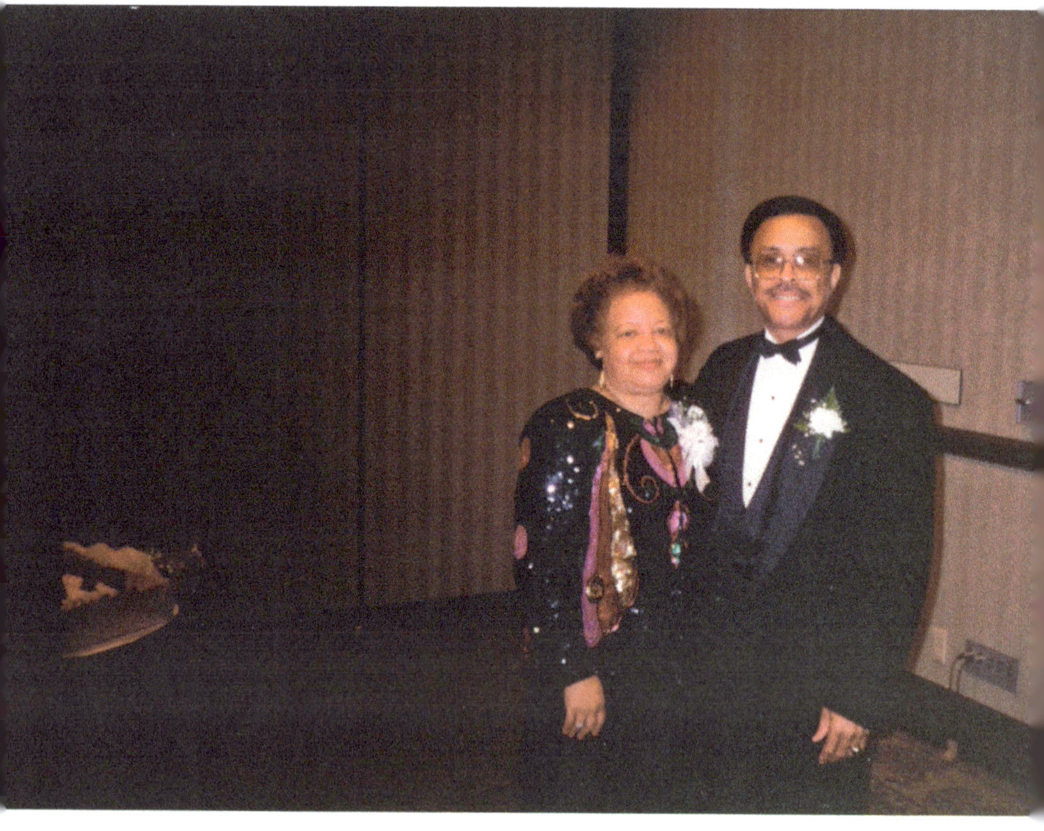

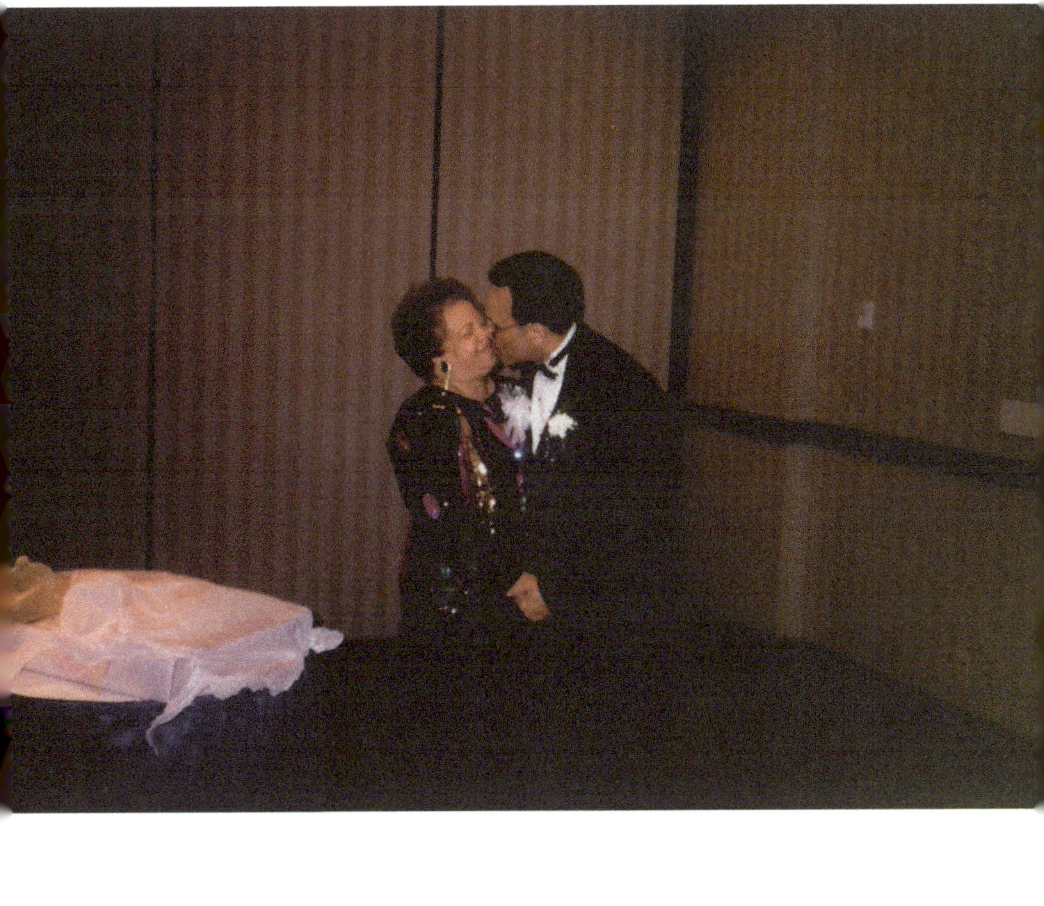

A picture of our oldest son Rawleigh W. Quarles, Jr. who was not available for either of the retirement dinners.

A SPECIAL THANK YOU TO

Mr. Roland H. Malone

Mrs. Betty A. Jones
Party Goods & More
301 24th Street, NW
Roanoke, Virginia 24017
(703) 343-2105

Mrs. Mary J. Waddell
One Design
Floral Arrangements

and

Mr. William W. (Bill) Field, Jr.
Mrs. Maxine N. Hunt
Dinner Music

Programs by Mary Lee Watkins Cabbler

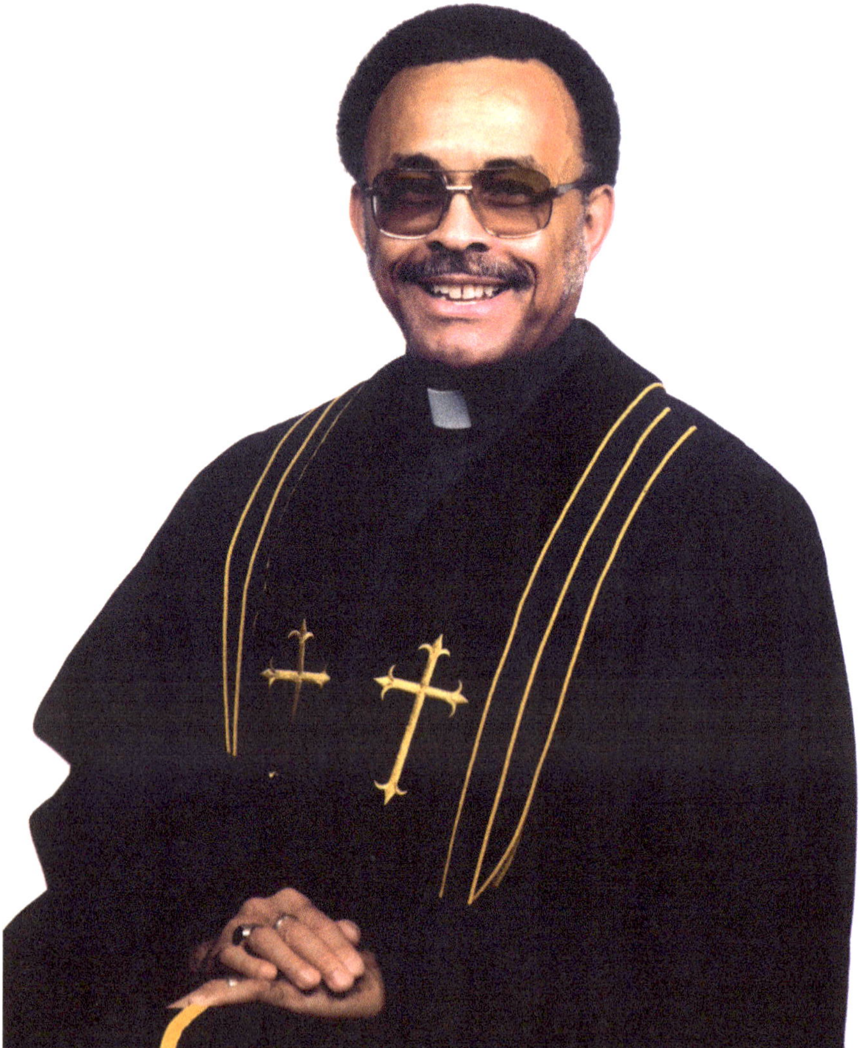

CHAPTER **14**

After Reaching the Top, What Now?! The Best Was Yet to Come!

I was divinely called of God to the preaching ministry in 1993. After my transition from Fire Chief to that of pastor, my primary focus had exceeded the preservation of life, the protection of property from the ravages of fire to that of the salvation, and redemption of the souls of mankind from sin. Quite a contrast, wouldn't you say? I was even given the reputation of "being the man who used to extinguish fires to that of the man who is starting fires." Even as a guest speaker for other churches, that's how I was sometimes introduced.

When I reflect back on how God had richly blessed me to become the fire chief, how He had guided and directed my steps in my career path, how He had permitted me by His grace and mercy to climb the ladder of success to reach my journey to the top, I often thought it strange and sometimes still do, that now after the victory was the Lord's and that the battle had been hard fought and won, why God would now lead me in pursuit of a different ministry or career.

As a fully surrendered child of God, I said yes to His divine will and purpose for my life and wholeheartedly and without reservation acknowledged my calling to proclaim the Word of God! I have had no regrets for making this decision. When God is first and foremost in our lives, His will, not ours should always be done! We should always say "not my will Lord, but thine will be done."

One of the hardest and most trying and emotional experiences ever in my life was in 1994, one year after I started preaching the gospel. I was diagnosed with cancer, and I wondered why God would suffer me to have cancer after obeying His call on my life to the preaching ministry. My faith was tested again, and boy was this ever a test of my faith! My first sermon title after returning to church following surgery was, "Why Me; Why Not Me?!" I exercised my faith in God for my divine healing and continued to preach the gospel, while remaining faithful to God's calling and His Word. Are you ready for this? God completely healed me divinely as well as through surgery and to this day as of the writing of this book, I can say with assurance and the utmost confidence that I am cancer free. What a mighty God we serve! I give God all the glory, honor, and praise for the great things He has done in my life! Sometimes, God permits Christians to suffer sickness, pain, disease, affliction, suffering, and trouble in our life, in order to test our faith as well as our faithfulness. And remember, God is the potter, and we are the clay. He is molding us, making us, and refining us, after His will. Just like gold is purified by fire. To each of you that are reading this book, I want you to know that I am still a work in progress. God is still working on me. He is not finished with me yet. And never forget that the steps of a good man are ordered by the Lord. Our prayer should be, order my steps Lord in your Word.

I call your attention to chapter 4 in which I experienced a hostile attitude against me from two firefighters during my career. In retrospect, as I reflect on the association, I now realize that God had placed me in each of their lives, as well as placed them in my life so that I could exemplify Christ and glorify God, as well as reveal the love, grace, and forgiveness of our Heavenly Father.

I had the opportunity to reveal the love of God as well as the forgiveness of God toward these individuals during their sickness and ill health. God permitted me to minister to them and serve each of them during their hospital stay as well as in their homes. It was a humbling experience for me to pray with them and share the love of God and the Word of God. See how God works! Yes, "He works in mysterious ways, His wonders to perform." I had the opportunity to attend the passing of one of the individuals and the privilege of delivering the eulogy. I was also privileged to visit with family and friends during family visitation at the passing of the other individual. I am so grateful to have had the opportunity to have become a change agent in both of their lives before they departed this life.

I sincerely hope that this autobiography serves as an inspiration to each reader as you climb the ladder of success on your journey to the top. You will face obstacles, set-backs, discouragement, intentionally set pitfalls, disappointments, hinderances, difficulties, hurdles, obstructions, and stumbling blocks, just to name a few.

Always remember, in your attempt to reach the top and achieve your goal, that God may have a divine purpose for your life that may not be what you had planned for yourself. We may not understand His direction and His will, but Psalm 37:23 says, "the steps of a good man are ordered by the Lord: and he is delighted in his way." So then, my prayer is, and your prayer should be, order my steps Lord." Even when we think that we have reached the top from our perspective, God still lets us know sometimes that He's not finished with us yet, and that He has a higher calling for us.

God made it perfectly clear to me that, although I thought I had climbed the ladder of success and journeyed to the top and could not advance any further, He said, "I have a higher calling for you!" and did He ever! When we humble ourselves therefore under the mighty hand of God, He will exalt us in due time (or at the right time). 1 Peter 5:6.

There's no calling, occupation, pursuit, business, profession, or position of achievement that compares to the high calling of God to serve mankind than that of the divine call of God to proclaim the gospel of Jesus Christ. Bar none!

In your quest to achieve your struggle to reach the top, always remember that "it's not by strength, nor by might, but by my Spirit says the Lord." Zechariah 4:6. Also, the Word of God says, "for the battle is not yours, but God's." 2 Chronicles 20: 15b. Walk with God as you climb the ladder of success in your journey to the top.

After all that I've been through, I'm still standing! God has been my refuge, my buckler and shield, my strength, and a very present help in trouble. If it had not been for the Lord who was on my side! May God richly bless each of you is my prayer. God loves you.

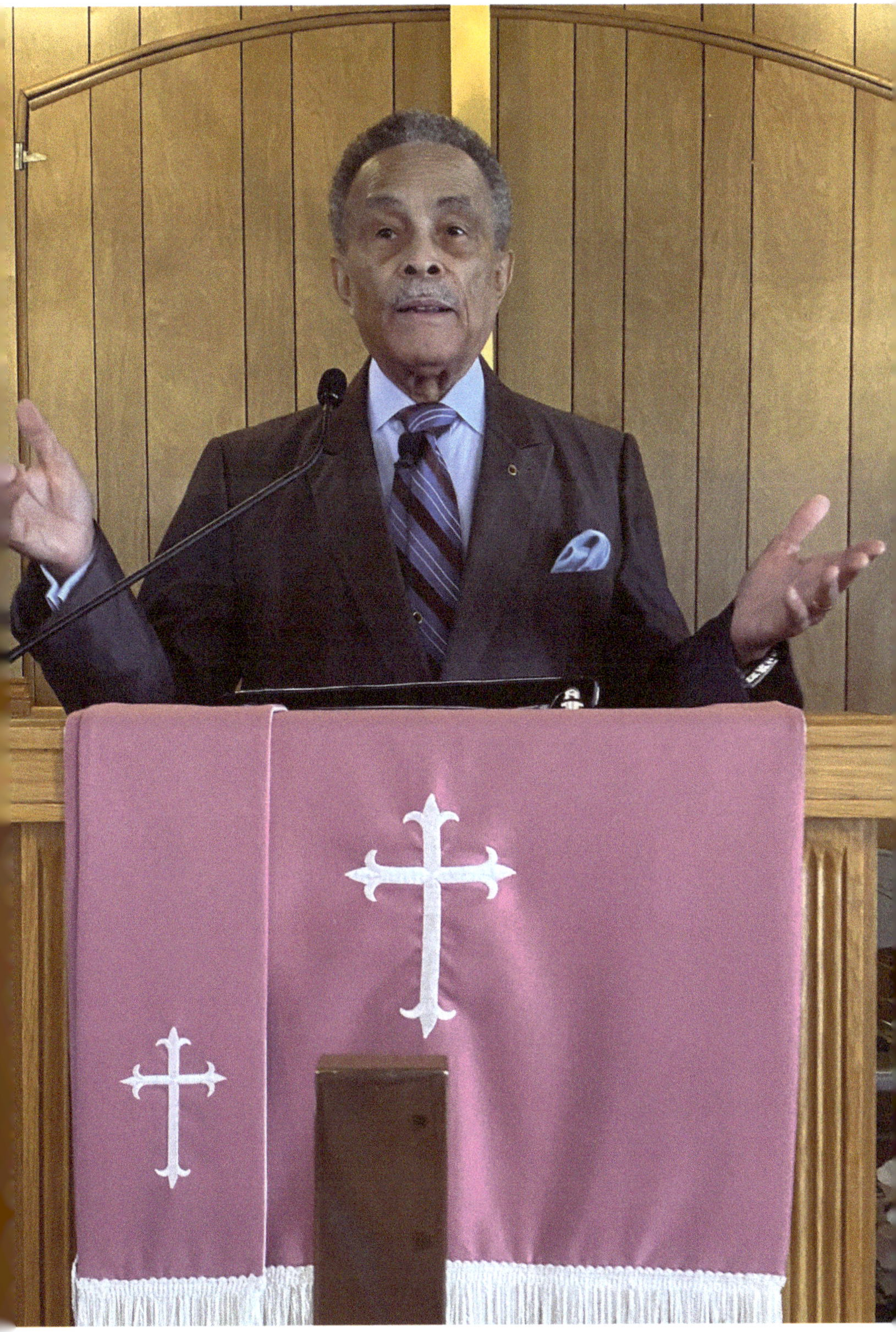

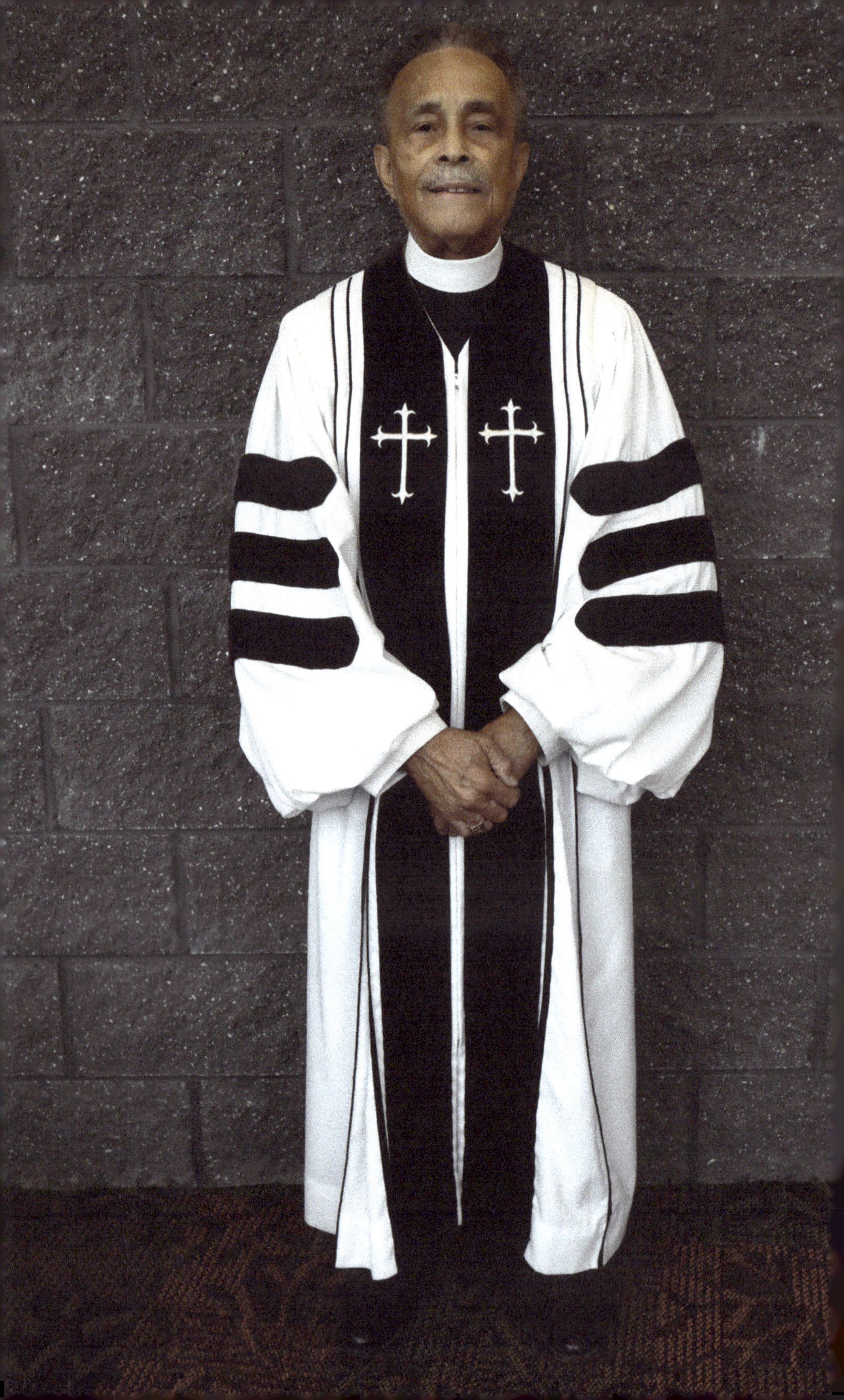

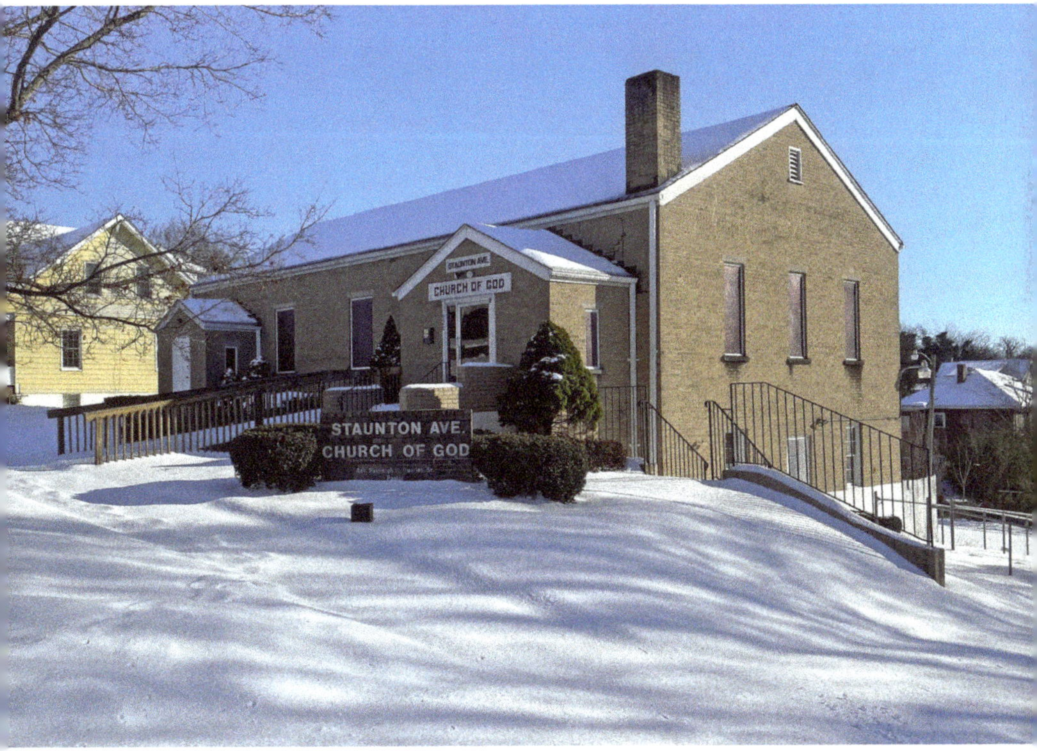
STAUNTON AVE.
CHURCH OF GOD
STAUNTON AVE.
CHURCH OF GOD

STAUNTON AVE. CHURCH OF GOD

Rev. Rawleigh W. Quarles, Sr.
Pastor

CPSIA information can be obtained
at www.ICGtesting.com
Printed in the USA
LVHW071120180922
728596LV00015B/151/J